THE ECONOMICS OF ENVIRONMENTAL IMPROVEMENT

THE ECONOMICS
OF ENVIRONMENTAL IMPROVEMENT

Donald T. Savage

Melvin Burke

John D. Coupe

Thomas D. Duchesneau

David F. Wihry

James A. Wilson

University of Maine, Orono

HOUGHTON MIFFLIN COMPANY   BOSTON

Atlanta   Dallas   Geneva, Illinois   Hopewell, New Jersey   Palo Alto   London

Printed in the U.S.A.

Library of Congress Catalog Card Number: 73-14497

ISBN: 0-395-18146-1

Contents

Preface

One of the problems of teaching or studying economics is the tendency to compartmentalize economic problems. In most introductory courses, various price theory problems are analyzed using the tools of price theory. Then, macroeconomic theory is presented and various macroeconomic problems are considered. Each subfield of economics is treated as a separate unit with its own problem areas. Too often, the student does not learn to appreciate the interrelationships between these subfields, and he is left with a collection of imperfectly connected ideas. The economic analysis of environmental problems offers a unique opportunity to improve the teaching of economics by providing an understanding of the complex interrelationships of the economic system.

The complete analysis of environmental economics draws upon the full range of economic concepts. For example, the cost of pollution abatement by a firm provides a method for illustrating basic price theory. The implications of environmental improvement provide a vehicle by which to illustrate the effects of both the investment and the government expenditures on the determination of the aggregate level of income and employment.

This book is an attempt to achieve four goals. First, the authors wanted to provide the student with the broadest possible coverage of the economic problems involved in improving the quality of the environment. Second, the authors have used the environmental issue to promote a greater understanding of the interrelations within the economy and between the various branches of economics. Third, by using the talents of several economists, each of whom could study the relationships between environmental economics and his areas of special interest, greater depth of coverage was made possible. Fourth, the above goals were to be achieved at a level that would be understandable by undergraduate students equipped with only a current or past introductory economics course.

Use of this text is possible in three types of courses. First, it can be employed as a supplement in Principles of Economics. Here it will serve as an example of the application of a wide range of economic concepts to a current problem. Second, a deeper discussion of environmental economics in a Problems of Economics type course could be based upon this book—with other readings being added depending on the amount of time being devoted to this issue. Third, the student in the intermediate level Environmental Economics course will find the book a good point at which to begin to delve into the full analysis of the problem.

The writing of the book presented all of the problems which should have been, but were not, thought of in considering a six-man effort. The project began with an outline which was done and redone several times as reviewer comments were received. Each author had the basic responsibility for the content of his chapter or chapters within the overall outline. In addition, each author read, criticized, and edited chapters written by the other authors. Dr. Donald T. Savage acted as coordinator of the project and did the initial editing of the manuscript.

While the book is a unit, rather than a collection of essays, the chapter, or chapters, produced by each author are their own creations. The individual authors were responsible for the following chapters:

Dr. Donald T. Savage: Chapters 1, 6, and 12
Dr. Melvin Burke: Chapter 7
Dr. John D. Coupe: Chapters 2 and 4
Dr. Thomas D. Duchesneau: Chapters 3 and 10
Dr. David F. Wihry: Chapters 8, 9, and 11
Dr. James A. Wilson: Chapter 5

The authors wish to thank a large number of individuals who assisted in the writing of this book. First, we are grateful to the staff at Houghton Mifflin for their assistance and guidance during the writing and production process. Professor Frank Egan of Trinity

College and Professor Frank J. Convery of Duke University provided thoughtful reviews of the manuscript. In addition, other anony-
mous reviewers who criticized earlier drafts provided valuable help
in the final design of the product. We wish to thank Ms. Jennifer
Albright, Secretary to the Department of Economics at the University
of Maine at Orono for her typing assistance. Finally, we must ac-
knowledge the assistance of several student assistants: Ms. Nancy
Graham, Ms. Meredyth Breed, Ms. Laurie Benton, Ms. Karen Bye, and
Ms. Marie Bourque, who spent countless hours typing various chapter drafts.

Donald T. Savage
Melvin Burke
John D. Coupe
Thomas D. Duchesneau
David F. Wihry
James A. Wilson

Orono, Maine

Part One

MARKET FAILURE AND RESOURCE
REALLOCATION

1

Introduction

The problem of improving the environment is at once social, scientific, academic, and economic. The quality of the environment is a social issue because it forces the individual to question the relationship between the institutions of society and the environment. Can a modern society be organized in a manner compatible with the preservation of the environment? Specifically, does the organization of modern American society mean that the environment eventually will be rendered incapable of supporting human life? If the present organization of society is not appropriate, what changes in social institutions would be conducive to effective environmental preservation?

Of prime socioeconomic importance is the degree of public willingness to sacrifice additional goods and services in order to devote additional resources to restoring the environment. Will consumers sacrifice individual economic self-interest for the social goods of better air and water? For example, will the housewife buy a higher priced, nonpolluting detergent in order to protect the nation's water or will she purchase the lower priced, polluting detergent at the expense of the quality of America's waterways? Decisions of this sort will be of crucial importance in the eventual success or failure of attempts to improve the environment. A fundamental question is whether American society encourages individuals to make choices for the well-being of the whole society or whether American society requires extensive controls to force socially beneficial choices?

The scientific implications of the environmental question are clear. Will society devote enough resources to scientific research to make possible the production of goods and the disposal of waste without environmental damage? Is technology sufficiently advanced to repair the damage already done? For example, can mercury deposits be removed from a river? Science must develop methods of avoiding future damage to the quality of the environment and systems for correcting past errors.

The problem of environmental improvement involves a closer relationship among agriculture, engineering, and the physical, natural, and social sciences. For example, it is of little use if the economist proposes a solution calling for technology which is outside the range of scientific capabilities. Environmental improvement requires the lowering of interdisciplinary barriers in the academic world in order that the points of view of many fields can be focused on the problems.

As an economic problem, environmental change is unique. Nearly all of the areas of specialization within economics can contribute to its analysis. Price theory and public finance are critical, but national income analysis, economic development, industrial organization, and labor economics are also important.

This book is concerned with only that part of the total effort to improve the environment which falls within the discipline of economics. Political aspects, engineering problems, and other parts of the whole effort will be considered only as they relate to economic concerns. The main chapters examine the important economic factors from the points of view of specialists in the various areas of economics. This introductory section discusses the general considerations which lead to the more technical analysis.

What Is Pollution?

Pollution consists of consumption and production by-products which either adversely affect the senses or physical well-being of a significant proportion of a given population or act to reduce the real or potential output of other goods. This definition requires some explanation and examples.

First, pollution can be created either by the production or the consumption of goods. The smoke from a factory is an obvious example of pollution; yet the consumption of phosphate detergents by the housewife also creates pollution.

Second, while pollution frequently is encountered through the use of the human sense organs — the eye, ear, nose, and mouth — there are forms of pollution which are not perceived by these organs. Our physical health is affected by mercury pollution in water and lead deposits in the air even though our senses do not detect the presence of these contaminants.

Third, a phenomenon cannot be considered pollution if it affects only a small proportion of the group which potentially could be affected. The tastes of one individual may be so different from those of the group that he regards as offensive the existence of a condition which would not disturb the average person.

Fourth, while we tend to think of pollution in the context of a negative interaction with our senses or health, it is also necessary to consider the effect of pollution on the actual or potential output of other goods. For example, the pollution of coastal waters reduces the real output of shellfish and the careless cutting of forests reduces the potential output of lumber.

Finally, pollution is not limited to water, air, and land; it includes noise pollution, urban congestion pollution, and visual pollution.

Why Is the Environment Polluted?

Every day the press reports the discovery of new damage to the environment. The daily papers tell us that another chemical has been found to be persistent, another wild animal has dangerously high concentrations of pesticides in its body, or another lake has been closed to recreational use because of bacterial pollution. Each year it becomes more difficult to find places where it is safe to swim, safe to breathe the air, safe to eat the fish or game, and safe to drink the water. Are we destroying ourselves in our attempts to produce more goods?

At the start of this inquiry into the economic aspects of environmental improvement, it is worthwhile to examine the process by which we reached this state of environmental degradation.

The Measurement of Output Gross national product — the measure of the market value of the output of final goods and services produced by the economy in a year — is the most widely used measure of economic activity. GNP changes are watched carefully by business, government, investors, and the general public. We have, however, been watching a misleading index. Gross national product measures the market value of goods and services produced but it does not deduct all the costs resulting from the production of those goods and services. For example, the production of more cars increases gross national product, but the new cars also increase the level of air pollution. While the welfare gain — an individual's subjective evaluation of his own well-being — represented by the increased number of cars is counted as a plus factor in gross national product, the welfare loss resulting from added air pollution is not counted as a negative factor in gross national product. In discussing pollution we are concerned with the negative effects of production. There are positive effects which are excluded or included in the GNP at less than their full value. For example, government services are included at their cost to the government. The market value of these services might be higher or lower than the government's production cost. For example, if the government establishes a free public park, the cost of providing for the park is included in the GNP. If the park were privately owned and users were charged an admission fee, GNP would include the admission revenue less the cost to the owner of purchasing materials from other firms. If the contribution to gross national product resulting from private ownership were greater than the government's cost, then GNP would be understated; if the contribution to GNP from private ownership were less than the government's cost, then gross national product would be overstated. The admission charge does not completely measure welfare. The user of the park may experience a large welfare gain for a relatively small admission price. His welfare would best be measured by calculating the maximum amount he would be willing to pay rather than the actual amount he pays. GNP, then, does not measure our welfare, and our tendency to equate increases in GNP with increases in welfare has contributed to the increase of pollution.

Economists have attempted to devise theoretical measures which would accurately calculate the welfare of society but thus far these attempts have failed. First, there is no unit of measurement for welfare. How can the pleasure which a person receives from the ownership of a new car be measured? How can the displeasure caused by smog-irritated eyes be calculated? Clearly, there is no scientific way of quantifying either pleasure or pain. Second, different people may receive different amounts of pleasure from the same good. For example, one person may receive a great deal of pleasure from the ownership of a new automobile while another would receive a very low amount of pleasure from the ownership of that same automobile. Similarly, one person may be able to endure irritated eyes with much less displeasure than another. We cannot quantify pleasure and pain in terms of absolute units, and therefore we cannot compare one person's pleasure or pain with another's. Thus, society and economists, unable objectively to evaluate pleasure and pain, have measured these values in terms of dollars of output.

The emphasis on the dollar value of output has led to the inclusion of those items having a dollar price — the automobile, for example — and the exclusion of those items which are not sold and thus have no dollar price — eye irritation, for example.

Why have we concentrated on measuring the production of goods without any regard for the negative effects on the environment? The answer in part reflects American concern with economic growth. The United States has established as one of its goals the continual increase in the amount of output per capita. This is certainly a worthwhile goal. Economic growth produces more products for more consumers and permits an increase in the material standards of living. It is argued that economic growth is necessary for the elimination of poverty and other social problems in the United States. Furthermore, in the fifties and sixties many believed that rapid growth in the United States would encourage other less developed nations to adopt capitalistic economic systems. The growth race of the fifties and early sixties is an illustration of this justification of an emphasis on economic growth. However, society forgot that the measurement of growth — gross national product — did not include as negative values the negative effects of growth.

Traditional American Neglect of Natural Resources Americans never have had much concern for the effect of economic activity on nature. This historical disregard for the environment may stem from the fact that the ratio of population to land space was extremely low for much of our history. The colonists began a tradition of neglect of the soil that has persisted in our national thinking. Given such an immense quantity of land, there appeared to be little need for the preservation of its productivity. Farming could be carried on most effectively by using up the resources of the land and then abandoning that land for new, previously uncultivated land. Why preserve the quality of a given piece of land when there was a seemingly inexhaustible supply of land lying to the west? The movement of agriculture from the Atlantic Coast westward resulted in part from the need to replace depleted soil. Other resources of the young nation were treated with equal carelessness. The forests of the Northern Midwest were cut down with no thought given to the reforestation of the area. New trees to the west were waiting to be cut; the supply was unlimited.

The nations of Europe, on the other hand, did not develop attitudes of neglect, because in modern European history land and natural resources never appeared to be overabundant. It was always necessary to consider the replenishment of the soil and forests because the supply was known to be limited.

The American attitude of neglect extended to the disposal of waste products from homes and industries. The nearest, cheapest (in terms of dollars of immediate expense) system was the best system. Urban and industrial waste was discharged into rivers, lakes, oceans, and the atmosphere with no concern for the overall impact on the quality of the environment. Only in recent years has the public begun to realize the effects of its past policies and to demand some of the changes which are necessary if the quality of the environment is to be improved.

Pollution and National Income Levels Pollution appears to increase more than proportionately with increases in income. A poor, agricultural economy will not pollute its environment as much as a rich, industrialized economy. The poor economy cannot afford a high ratio of cars to people, and therefore air pollution is partially avoided. The industrial wastes of the primarily agrarian society are negligible because there is little industry. A rich society uses electric power to operate a multiplying supply of household appliances and conveniences that the poor society cannot afford. The generation of power to produce and operate these products of affluence contributes to pollution.

The poorer economy will be less polluted than the affluent economy because the poor economy is less industrialized, generally less urbanized, less likely to use large quantities of manufactured fertilizers, and less able to afford disposable products. On the other side, the poor economy may be more polluted because of the lack of funds to control the existing sources of pollution. For example, existing urban areas are frequently congested and have grown faster than the ability to control pollution sources. It would be reasonable to assume that rising levels of income in the less developed nations will bring rising levels of pollution unless economic development plans are such that adequate safeguards against pollution are provided.

Increase in Population Concentration The level of pollution is probably more a function of population density than of the absolute size of the population. The environment is able to absorb the wastes of a geographically dispersed society, but when most of the population is concentrated in urban areas, environmental problems are greatly intensified. For example, the sewage from isolated farms located along a river can be assimilated by the river. If instead of widely dispersed farms, however, the population is concentrated into a city which dumps its wastes into that same river, pollution becomes a problem. The higher the population density, the greater the burden put on the river at one point.

The city, by its very nature, both creates and concentrates sources of pollution. Because the city is a center of economic activity, there is industrial pollution as well as pollution resulting from the concentration of a large number of people in a limited area.

Industrial Competition In some ways competition between firms may have contributed to our present pollution problems. Competition, to the economist, implies production at the lowest possible cost. If the costs of preventing air or water pollution can be avoided, a firm can compete with its rivals more effectively. If one firm incurs the cost necessary to avoid pollution, that firm is less able to compete with firms which operate without regard to environmental damage. Thus, the concerned firm is at a competitive disadvantage. If all firms are required to incur the costs of pollution control, then no firm has a competitive handicap. In the absence of uniform rules regulating water and air quality, the competitive advantage may go to those firms doing the most damage to the environment.

Locational Competition and Development Problems The competition between geographical areas for new industry has contributed to environmental deterioration. If one state or city attempts to impose air or water quality standards on a polluting firm, the firm has been able to escape the antipollution costs by moving to a city or state less concerned about environmental problems. Areas with chronic unemployment may be tempted to trade environmental quality for additional employment. Thus, the differences in air and water quality standards between political areas act as constraints on areas considering more restrictive antipollution regulations.

The conflict between the desire to increase local employment and the desire to avoid environmental damage is clearly illustrated by the proposal to build an oil refinery and related petrochemical facilities along the coast of Maine. One faction argues that the cost of the new industry will be oil spillages and other environmental losses. Industries such as fishing and tourism may lose more income than will be generated by the new industries. The other faction believes that the gains in terms of fostering economic development and employment will be worth the increased risks of damage and that part of the price of industrial development is some loss of environmental quality.

Increased Use of Water and Chemicals   The growth of the economy and the pace of technological change have increased our use of water and chemicals. The discovery of increasingly complex chemical products in the past century has certainly been a great scientific achievement. Like most advances in technology, however, the gains of the chemical industry have not come without costs. As chemical production and consumption increase, chemical wastes also increase. Unfortunately, industry and consumers traditionally have discharged wastes into the air or water. The growth in chemical output and the increasing complexity of chemical compounds have increased the burden on the rivers and lakes.

The advances in chemistry have contributed to the spectacular increase in American agricultural productivity. Never in the history of man have so few farmers satisfied the food needs of so many. The chemicals used by the farmers as fertilizers, pesticides, and disease preventatives have not all been retained by the soil but instead have drained from the land into lakes and rivers. Some of these chemicals, such as DDT, do not break down in water and persist for years in the ecology of the river. The fish of the river absorb the chemicals. Thus, one part of the food supply is contaminated as a result of increases in the output of another part of the food supply.

Competition Between Public and Private Goods   Part of the environmental problem results from a failure to invest in public antipollution projects. Not all pollution is the result of private economic activity; much environmental damage is the result of the failure of cities and towns to invest in facilities such as sewage treatment plants and waste disposal plants.

Expanding on John Kenneth Galbraith's argument,[1] we can say that public antipollution efforts, like the production of other public goods and services, have been neglected in favor of private consumer goods and services. Galbraith's hypothesis that there is affluence in the private sector of the economy and poverty in the public sector seems to fit this case well.

All the preceding conditions have contributed to our present pollution problem. We cannot accurately or productively apportion the blame among them. We can, however, consider some of the results of society's behavior with regard to the environment and attempt to determine which groups have gained or lost, or both, because of past neglect of the environment.

The Winners and the Losers

Who have been the winners and the losers from increasing environmental pollution? Actually, everyone has both won and lost as a result of the pollution of the environment. Business firms have been able to avoid, or postpone, the costs of installing expensive air and water treatment facilities. But business cost savings do not automatically become business profits. The cost savings achieved have been shared by company stockholders through higher dividends and retained earnings, by company employees through higher wages, and by consumers of the product through lower prices. Thus, the cost savings have been distributed by the price mechanism to capital, labor, and the consumer. Not all business firms have gained from the lack of pollution control. Those firms dependent upon a reliable source of clean water as a raw material for their product, for example, have been subjected to higher costs, and these costs have been reflected in the price to consumers and in the returns to laborers and stockholders.

The consumer-taxpayer-property owner has gained from lack of environmental control in a number of ways. As a consumer he has been able to purchase many products at prices which have not reflected the full cost of their production. The user of paper, for example, has not paid the full cost of the production of the paper because some of the costs — especially those of abating air and water pollution — have been avoided by the producing firm. As a taxpayer the average citizen has gained because his taxes have been lower than they would have been if public facilities for the prevention of pollution had been constructed. As a property owner he has avoided the increased real estate taxes that would have been the most commonly used method of financing local waste disposal and sewage treatment facilities.

Thus, the gains from pollution have been relatively widespread. Those who argue that the owners of industries that produce pollution have been the sole beneficiaries of lax antipollution regulations do not understand the workings of the system. While pollution producers have benefited financially, so, in the short run, has society.

On the other side of the issue, the losses from environmental pollution probably have been even more widespread than the gains. The difference between the gains and the losses is that most of the gains are monetary benefits, while most of the losses are either nonmonetary or difficult to measure in money terms.

The monetary losses are incurred by those industries dependent upon a clean environment. The fishing industry in the Great Lakes incurs losses from pollution, and the recreation industries suffer as recreational areas become polluted. These are financial losses which can be measured in dollar terms.

In some cases we pay higher prices and producers incur higher costs because of our past failure to protect the environment. The price of our water supply would be lower if water did not need such extensive treatment before being biologically safe. The cost of a summer home at a lake is inflated by the fact that many lakes which could be developed are too polluted for recreational use. A potential developer must either seek a clean lake or incur the added costs of cleaning up a polluted lake. In either event, the consumer pays a higher price.

A final set of costs resulting from environmental pollution includes the impact of environmental deterioration on the value of existing properties. To take an extreme example, assume a person builds a house in an undeveloped, unzoned area. A year later, a firm builds a plant next to the house and the plant's production process discharges "rotten egg gas" into the air. The wind carries the odor into the person's house. Needless to say, the market value of the property has decreased because of the reduction in the quality of the environment. For people living in industrial areas, this sort of loss is very important. The market value of houses in entire neighborhoods or even entire towns may be decreased by the existence of one polluter. As another example of the effect of pollution on property values, consider the person who builds a summer home on a clean river or lake. A firm later locates a plant on the river or lake and causes water pollution. Naturally, the deterioration of the water quality lowers the market value of the land and home.

Other losses from environmental damage are more difficult to measure. We do not know how many man-hours of labor have been lost or dollars spent on illnesses resulting from air and water pollution. We do not know how man's expected life span has been changed by the build-up in his body of chemical pesticides. Indeed, it is conceivable that the pollution of the environment threatens the organic survival of the human race. Less dramatic are the esthetic losses caused by foul smelling air and drinking water which has been heavily chlorinated to kill bacteria. The loss of fresh, clean air cannot be given a dollar value but it is a loss nevertheless.

The above examples should be sufficient to illustrate the fact that everyone, either directly or indirectly, is affected by the existence of environmental pollution. Each individual may not receive losses equal to gains but each one receives gains and losses from environmental deterioration. In any case, it is safe to say that for each individual instance of pollution a redistribution of real income takes place. Likewise, pollution abatement will give rise to a redistribution of income. Since the distribution of income is often a very important social question, it is necessary that the benefits and costs resulting from changes in the distribution of income be considered in the analysis of any particular pollution abatement scheme.

The Environment as an Economic Problem

Some of the relationships between the environment and economics should be fairly clear from the preceding discussion. In this section the relationships are stated more specifically and the approach of the text is outlined.

Part One of the text deals with two problems. First, the price system is considered as a resource allocation device and the critical problem of market failure is introduced. Market failure is a condition in which the price of a good does not reflect all of the costs and benefits associated with the production and consumption of that good. The causes and consequences of market failure are considered in relation to the pollution problem. Second, the direct costs of pollution abatement are considered. Clearly, the cost of abating pollution will be both high and unevenly distributed between industries. Third, the methods by which the costs of pollution abatement can be imposed upon the polluters are described. Finally, the ultimate incidence of the costs of pollution abatement is discussed. The firm which is forced to accept added costs may be able, through the price mechanism, to pass those costs forward to its customers or backwards to the factors of production.

Part Two examines a series of constraints on policy design. While society desires environmental improvement, there are other important goals which society may not be willing to sacrifice. These constraining factors have to be considered as sources of potential trade-offs with environmental improvement.

The first chapter of Part Two considers the question of whether those suffering losses of either human or physical capital should be compensated for their losses. Does society have an obligation to compensate the worker who loses his factory job when the plant closes as a result of stricter environmental legislation? Should the owner of the plant be compensated for his loss? The second chapter is devoted to consideration of the macroeconomic objectives of employment and prices. Will the level of employment increase or decrease as a result of environmental improvement? What will be the effect on the general price level? In the third chapter consideration is given to the potential conflict between environmental improvement and economic growth. Must society give up growth goals in order to have a decent environment?

Part Three critically examines current environmental policies. It examines theoretically the role of government in pollution control and reviews past and pending legislation. The theory of, and experience with, nonmarket policy techniques is evaluated. Have policy programs using regulation of industry worked in the past? Will regulation be able to deal with the environmental problem?

Part Four considers market oriented environmental policies such as a charge on effluents. Will programs operating through the price system lead to greater environmental gains than the nonmarket approaches such as regulation? The final chapter summarizes the key points of the analysis and presents conclusions and recommendations.

2

The Market System and the Environment

The study of the economics of environmental improvement begins with an understanding of the nature of an economic system, because the basic cause of environmental problems is a specific type of market system failure. The first section of this chapter reviews the goals of a market system, identifies the relationships between allocative efficiency and environmental problems, and indicates the effect of environmental improvement on the achievement of the system's other goals. The following sections of the chapter trace the development of the literature dealing with market failure and present increasingly complex models of the economic aspects of environmental problems.

The Economic System

All economic systems are concerned with four central goals: efficiency, equity, stability, and growth. Efficiency and equity are related to the processes of production and consumption and are considered under the heading of microeconomics. Stability and growth are associated with the overall performance of an economy and are considered under the heading of macroeconomics. These four goals are closely related to one another and cannot be considered separately either for the undertaking of economic analysis or for the formulation of economic policies.

Alternative forms of economic organization, such as capitalism, socialism, and fascism, provide different mechanisms for attaining economic goals. The study of comparative economic systems is beyond the scope of this book; this chapter concerns one type of economic organization, the American form of mixed capitalism.

Efficiency   In the American economy, allocation decisions are made through a complex system of markets for goods and for factors of production. Perfect efficiency in the market allocation of resources exists if all goods are being produced at the lowest possible cost and if the composition of total output is such that consumer welfare cannot be improved by any change in the output mix.

The overriding question concerns the conditions which must exist so that economic efficiency will result if *all* production and consumption decisions are to be resolved by the market. First, there must be pure competition in all markets. This condition would prevent any single seller or buyer from having even the slightest control over the price of products or over the returns to the factors of production. Second, the market must be capable of producing all goods desired by consumers. Under this condition, there are no collective (public) goods. Individuals would meet all their needs — including those of defense and education — by market purchases. Third, firms must be faced with increasing costs at an output level very small in relation to the total market for the product. This condition would insure a large number of firms in each industry. In other words, high concentration or monopolization of an industry must not be economically feasible. Fourth, there must be perfect knowledge and perfect mobility. Perfect knowledge insures that all desires and all responses to changes in desires are recorded in the market. Perfect mobility insures that resources can be easily reallocated in response to market pressures.

Finally, allocative efficiency requires that all costs and benefits must be registered in the marketplace. This is a *critical* condition for the development of the analysis of environmental economics. Environmental damage has resulted because all costs have not been recorded in the marketplace. For example, the price of an automobile does not include the costs of air pollution, health care, smog damage to crops, and general discomfort, all of which result from the production and use of automobiles.

The restrictiveness of the conditions necessary for economic efficiency is self-evident. None of these conditions are met in the real world and compensatory action is necessary to approximate efficiency conditions. Compensatory action in the United States has taken the form of government involvement in the economy. Antitrust laws have been enacted in an attempt to maintain competition. Government provides such collective goods as national defense, public highways, and police and fire protection. Immunization programs are publicly funded. Government regulation of pollution and the funding of sewage treatment plants result from the recognition of the unmeasured costs of production.

Equity   Individuals own resources and make them available for use in the production process. In the absence of government action, the distribution of resource ownership among individuals would dictate the distribution of income. If the initial distribution of resource ownership had been equitable when the economic organization was established and if the ownership pattern had generated and maintained equity over time, economists could ignore this characteristic of an economy. Equity considerations, particularly income distribution, are not built into economic organizations and compensatory government action is necessary. Unfortunately, economists have not developed a viable theory of income distribution; hence, equity considerations and government action have been formulated piecemeal. Welfare programs at the local level, mixed Federal and state programs such as old age assistance, and different minimum wages at the state and Federal level are examples of the piecemeal approach to equity. Also, equity considerations are built into the structure of taxation and, to some extent, into decisions about government expenditure. The most recent attempts to correct inequities are embodied in President Johnson's "War on Poverty" programs and President Nixon's proposed welfare reforms.

Correction of existing environmental problems involves consideration of equity issues. The value of human and physical resources will be affected by changes in environmental regulations. If the polluting paper mill is forced to close, the employees and owners will both lose. The employees will lose their jobs and may be forced to go on welfare, to move to a new location, or to accept a lower paying job with another firm. The owners of the firm will find that the market value of their investment has declined drastically and that the income from their investment has decreased to zero. Neither the owners nor the employees will consider this redistribution of income equitable.

Stability   Past fluctuations in the United States economy demonstrate that the economic system tends to be unstable rather than stable. Hence, "Keynesian economics," with its emphasis on monetary and fiscal policy adjustments, has gained broad acceptance. These macroeconomic policies, along with other microeconomic policies, are needed to achieve full employment and price stability.

Environmental improvement has implications for economic stability. Obviously, pollution abatement requires large capital investment and imposes new capital and operating costs upon firms. A change in either total investment or the composition of total investment presents a threat to the macroeconomic stability of the system. A sudden increase in investment could cause inflation; a cessation of investment could cause a recession. Any examination of environmental economics must concern itself with these possible complications.

Growth All economic systems must provide a mechanism for achieving economic growth. The production of capital goods results in higher future production of consumer goods. As long as the rate of growth in real output exceeds the rate of population growth, standards of living improve.

Even though growth occurs within the framework of a market economy, the rate of growth may not be acceptable. Hence, the Federal government acts to influence the rate of growth. Patent laws are enacted to stimulate invention, tax laws are used to promote the creation of capital goods, and interest rates are adjusted to encourage or retard investment. In macroeconomics, the role of government in promoting stability and growth is preeminent.

The growth goal has come under attack by the environmentalists. Growth, the environmentalists say, means more pollution, a faster depletion of natural resources, less open space, and a general decline in the quality of life. Never before has the value of growth been placed in such great doubt.

The process of correcting and preventing environmental abuses also threatens society's ability to achieve a high rate of growth. The more productive capacity must be used for pollution abatement equipment, the less it can be used for other products. Society may be faced with a choice between the acquisition of consumer goods and the improvement of the environment.

The Development of the Theory of Market Failure

The environmental problem has developed because one of the conditions of allocative efficiency — that all costs and benefits be recorded in the market place — has not been met. Correction of the problem of allocative efficiency threatens the complete achievement of the other goals of the system — equity, stability and growth.

Public awareness of the environmental problem is a recent development. Given the magnitude and pervasiveness of the problem, as it is seen today, why was action not taken many years ago? Was it because there was no concern about or recognition of the problem? Was it because economists have not paid any attention to this problem?

The literature of economics has long been concerned with the issue of the market mechanism's failure to record all costs and benefits. Only recently, however, have these concepts been applied to environmental problems. Early works on market failure explained the possible divergence between social and private net product. Henry Sidgwick is credited with being the first economist to question the equality of social and private net product under a laissez-faire competitive system.[1] Sidgwick used the example of a lighthouse constructed by a shipowner to provide navigational assistance to his ships. In deciding to build the lighthouse, the shipowner was explicitly indicating that his benefits from the lighthouse would be greater than the costs of constructing and operating the lighthouse. Yet the lighthouse also provided benefits to other passing ships, and those ships did not pay for the navigational benefits which they received. Thus, social net product — the gain to all ships using the lighthouse — exceeded the private net product — the gain to the lighthouse owner. In modern terminology, marginal social product exceeded marginal private product.

Marginal private product is the gain in utility accruing to an individual as a result of the consumption of an additional unit of a product. The product will be consumed by the individual provided that the gain in utility exceeds the cost of the good.

Marginal social product is the gain in utility accruing to society as a result of the consumption of an additional unit of a product. The product should be created for society's use provided that this gain in utility exceeds the cost to society.

Sidgwick concluded that under private ownership too few lighthouses would be constructed and argued that government should provide such goods. Modern economists assert the need to provide public goods on the grounds that all benefits are not recorded in the marketplace.

A. C. Pigou elaborated Sidgwick's argument in the early part of the century:

I now turn to the second class of divergence between social and private net product which was distinguished in §3. Here the essence of the matter is that one person A, in the course of rendering some service, for which payment is made, to a second person B, incidentally also renders services or disservices to other persons (Not producers of like services), of such a sort that payment cannot be extracted from the benefited parties or compensation enforced on behalf of the injured parties.[2]

Pigou succinctly points out that, contrary to the assumptions of the laissez-faire competitive system, not all costs and benefits are recorded in the marketplace. Therefore, public goods are underproduced and private goods are overproduced. Pigou gives as an example of disservices to other persons the discharge of smoke from factory chimneys causing loss to the community in the form of damage to buildings, injury to crops, and additional cleaning expenses. He even cites the report of a committee investigating smoke damage in Pittsburgh in 1912 in which the cost of such damage was estimated at nearly twenty dollars per capita per annum.[3]

Using today's terminology, the discharge of smoke is an external diseconomy imposing a social cost which represents the divergence between marginal social benefit and marginal social cost. In perfect competition, price equals marginal cost and price also equals the marginal social valuation of an additional unit of product. If marginal private cost is equal to marginal social cost, then maximum social welfare occurs at the output level at which marginal social cost equals marginal social benefit. In the factory smoke example, marginal social cost is greater than marginal private cost and with profit maximization, price is equated to marginal private cost. Hence, marginal social cost exceeds marginal social benefit and maximum social welfare is not attained.

Therefore, if external economies or diseconomies exist, perfect competition does not result in maximum social welfare. According to one economist, "an external economy (diseconomy) is said to exist when marginal social cost is less than (is greater than) marginal social benefit." [4]

Scholarly debate in economics journals began shortly after the publication of Pigou's *Wealth and Welfare*.[5] For better or worse, the debate generated by Pigou never came to the public's attention. Other events — the depression of the 1930s and World War II — and other debates overshadowed its importance. Keynes' *General Theory of Employment, Interest and Money* and the development of models of imperfect competition by Chamberlain and Robinson commanded the attention of academics during the 1930s and 1940s. Immediately after World War II, macroeconomic problems continued to be the focus of economists' attention. Concern over postwar adjustment, potential unemployment, and the Full-Employment Act of 1946 gave way to concern over postwar inflation, yet attention remained on macroeconomic problems. Before all of these economic events could be put in perspective, the Cold War began and the Korean War followed. Journal articles focusing on the questions raised by Pigou reappeared in the 1950s. Two articles of particular importance are Bator's

"The Anatomy of Market Failure" and Coase's "The Problem of Social Cost." [6]

The term "externality" has been used to encompass the situations generating market failure. The need for this term is demonstrated by Bator's generalization of the problem:

In its modern version, the notion of external economies . . . belongs to a more general doctrine of "direct interaction." Such interaction, whether it involves producer-producer, consumer-consumer, producer-consumer, or employer-employee relations consists of interdependences that are external to the price system, hence unaccounted for by market valuations.[7]

The same reasoning applies to external diseconomies. Some authors use the terms "spill-over effects" or "neighborhood effects" instead of "externalities."

The literature demonstrates that economists have developed theories which contribute to an understanding of pollution. These theories have been concerned primarily with the generation of social costs and their consequences for the overall efficiency of the allocation of resources.

The problems associated with misallocations of resources were not brought to the public's attention until 1958, in John Kenneth Galbraith's *The Affluent Society*. Galbraith emphasized the lack of production of public goods in this affluent country:

The family which takes its mauve and cerise, air-conditioned, power-steered, and power-braked automobile for a tour passes through cities that are badly paved, made hideous by litter, blighted buildings, billboards, and posts for wires that should long since have been put underground. They pass on into a countryside that has been rendered largely invisible by commercial art. (The goods which the latter advertise have an absolute priority in our value system. Such aesthetic considerations as a view of the countryside accordingly come second. On such matters we are consistent.) They picnic on exquisitely packaged food from a portable icebox by a polluted stream and go on to spend the night at a park which is a menace to public health and morals. Just before dozing off on an air mattress, beneath a nylon tent, amid the stench of decaying refuse, they may reflect vaguely on the curious unevenness of their blessings. Is this, indeed, the American genius? [8]

Public awareness of the problems of externalities, particularly social costs, then, is a recent development.

Similar developments in other academic disciplines occurred at about the same time. The problems of population growth, poverty, and man's upsetting of the ecological balance added to the public focus on the quality of life. Actual events such as air pollution deaths in several cities, oil spills endangering coastlines, and wildlife deaths caused by pesticides reinforced the position of those pointing out the problem areas. Given the nation's affluence, society may now believe that it can afford to change its ways.

Imperfections and Efficiency Conditions

The previous section traced the historical development of the concepts of social costs and benefits. In the real world, other institutional and economic factors contribute to inefficiency. Among them are the concern for property rights, the imperfections of the market system, and the problem of mobility.

Property Rights   Recent developments in the theory of externalities have emphasized that the divergence of social and private costs is rooted in the problem of defining property rights. One of the basic components of a capitalist economic system is the existence of property rights. Economists are concerned with property rights because it is through the definition and exercise of property rights that the basis for exchange is established. The efficiency conditions assume that all property rights are vested and exercised. In most cases property rights are vested and exercised, and prices are established as a return to property owners.

The air and most bodies of water are not privately owned, so no one person can charge others for their use. They have become, *de facto,* common property. Furthermore, governments have failed to define ownership of common properties. Consequently, these common properties have been abused. Within the framework of the economic organization of this country, the maximum amount of a free good (common property uncontrolled by restrictions) is used in the process of production and consumption. The problems resulting from the abuse of common property are quite clear. The air is polluted; many rivers are polluted; and the ocean is on the verge of pollution. To further emphasize the plight of common property, as opposed to property for which rights are defined and exercised, we can note the fact that although there is no threat to the existence of domestic animals (private property), many species of wildlife (common property) are threatened with extinction.

Discharges from the public and private sectors of the economy are an extremely important source of the environmental problem. For example, DDT, chlorinated hydrocarbons, and a variety of other chemicals harm the common property into which they are discharged and impose a cost on society.

Threats to the environment from either the use of private, or the misuse of common, property must be quickly identified and dealt with if progress is to be made toward improving the environment.[9]

Market Imperfections Analysis of the environmental problem becomes more difficult when market imperfections are introduced. The model of pure competition assumes that neither product prices nor factor prices can be controlled by either buyers or sellers. It also assumes that firms must be faced with increasing costs at an output level very small in relation to the total market for the product. The result is a large number of firms in each industry so that high concentration or monopolization is not economically feasible.

These assumptions, however, do not always hold true in the real world. Under certain circumstances, the introduction of some degree of market control can aggravate the environmental problem. In a one factory town, the single employer may not be pressured to stop polluting the air because the citizens fear reprisals in the form of the loss of work. Firms in a highly concentrated industry may resist, through tacit agreement, engaging in environmental improvement. The action would be designed to hold costs as low as possible.

Mobility Effective market functioning also requires perfect mobility of resources. This condition insures that resources can be reallocated very easily in response to market pressures. The environmental problem is indirectly complicated when perfect mobility does not exist.

Under extreme conditions, environmental improvement could result in the closing of a plant. The unemployed workers may not have the mobility to obtain employment in another area. There are many examples of pockets of unemployment caused by structural changes in our economy. Perhaps the most publicized is the unemployment in Appalachia.

Efforts to improve the environment can cause structural changes in the economy. If the mobility condition is relaxed, then the solution to the environmental problem has another dimension.

Economic Views of the Environmental Problem

The failure to register all costs and benefits in the market has been partially responsible for the deterioration of the environment. If constraints had been imposed on the use of discharge mechanisms at the time of the Industrial Revolution, today's environmental problem would be minimal. The costs associated with discharges would be registered in the market and resources would have been used to produce goods to control discharges. Fewer consumer goods would have been produced and the production of capital goods for environmental preservation would have been greater. As a result, the rate of growth of output would have decreased. Whether we would be better or worse off today if these actions had been taken is a question to ponder.

An Oversimplified View Consider a single firm which in the course of production causes both air and water pollution. The costs of these contaminating discharges are not registered in the market. If they were recorded, the supply curve would shift. Each firm would offer a given quantity of product for sale at a higher price because its marginal cost curve would have been shifted. The aggregate effect on the industry supply curve is shown in Figure 2-1.

The unrecorded social costs would be C (per unit of production). From the viewpoint of economic efficiency, the market, as it is operating, causes a greater quantity to be produced at a lower price as compared to the equilibrium solution in which the social costs are introduced. As indicated earlier, these social costs take the form of burdens imposed on others. The polluted water cannot be used for fishing or recreation and the polluted air causes health problems and a generally obnoxious odor.

What conclusions can be drawn from this view of the problem? First, C exists and is a positive number, though it need *not* be the same as the abatement cost per unit. Second, if all currently unrecorded social costs were recorded in the marketplace, the supply

Figure 2-1

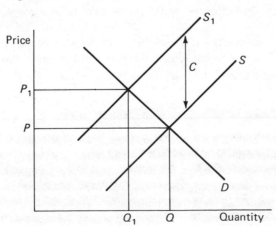

curve would be S_1 in Figure 2-1. Consequently, from society's view-point, a greater than socially optimal output is produced when all costs are not registered.

But we have yet to take equity considerations into account. Who are the gainers and who are the losers? The losers are the fishermen who can no longer fish in the river, the people who can no longer breathe fresh air, and the clam diggers and the clam consumers who suffer because the clam flats are polluted. The gainers are the consumers of the product who pay a lower price, the workers who benefit from the employment generated by the higher output level, and the other owners of the factors of production used in producing this product. Thus it is not entirely clear that society as a whole loses from the failure to account for social cost.

A More Complex View   The partial equilibrium analysis above gives an oversimplified view of the social costs and benefits involved in the environmental problem. The complexity of the problem can be illustrated by an example without constructing a detailed model. Consider the totality of the unmeasured costs of producing and consuming a newspaper. Merely to point to the paper mill as a source of pollution is misleading, because the mill represents only a small part of the problem.

Paper mills are generally located near the bulky primary raw material, trees. The process of incurring unmeasured costs begins in the forest when the trees are cut. Not all parts of the tree are used in papermaking; for example, bark is unusable and is discarded. Steel and other metals, glass, and wire were produced and embodied in the paper mill's equipment. Chemicals were produced and stored to be used in the production process. In each case vehicles had to transport the inputs to the mill. Steel, rubber, glass and fuels were produced to make and operate these vehicles. In other words, size-able unmeasured costs have been incurred before the mill produces any paper. The inputs are produced all over the country and at each of these production points there are a variety of side effects.

When paper production begins, one obvious input is energy. The major source of energy is electricity. The generation of power to produce the paper and all the prior inputs causes air and thermal pollution. The production of the paper itself causes discharges into the air and water. More unmeasured costs are incurred.

The intermediate product, newsprint, is transported to a variety of locations for further processing. The printing plant has a similar series of inputs in the building and equipment, together with inks, dyes, and chemicals to convert the newsprint into newspapers. Again, electrical energy is used in the process and the newspapers are stacked up for delivery.

More fuel-consuming vehicles are required to deliver the newspapers to the newsstands and homes. The process is still not at an end. Once read, the newspapers are disposed of in a variety of ways. Some are burned in incinerators, fireplaces, and dumps. Others are thrown out carelessly and become litter. Still others are recycled for use in producing different goods.

The unmeasured costs of producing a newspaper are myriad and incurred nationally. With population growth and an increasing demand for newspapers, the production of all inputs used in the production and consumption of newspapers must be expanded. Hence, the problems associated with unmeasured costs are dynamic and not static.

An Interindustry Analysis The relationships between industries, which were treated verbally in the newspaper example, can be analyzed formally by using input-output tables. The purpose of the input-output table is to quantify the transactions between the various sectors of manufacturing and the other sectors of the economy. A hypothetical input-output table is presented in Table 2-1. For simplicity, the table assumes an economy with only three industries and a household sector.

A horizontal reading of the data reveals the shipments of each industry's output. For example, Industry A ships $10 worth of its product to itself, $8 worth of product to Industry B, $4 of product to Industry C, and $6 of its product to households.

Table 2-1   Hypothetical Input-Output Table:
                 Purchasing Industry

	A Water polluter	B Air polluter	C Non- polluter	D Households	Total output
A (Water polluter)	10	8	4	6	28
B (Air polluter)	6	16	8	20	50
C (Nonpolluter)	8	12	4	6	30
D (Households)	4	14	14	10	42
Total Input	28	50	30	42	150

Reading vertically one obtains data on a given industry's purchases from other industries. For example, Industry A purchases $10 worth of product from itself, $6 worth of product from Industry B, $8 of product from Industry C, and $4 worth of factor inputs from households. Its total inputs, $28, are equal to its total outputs.

How does this type of table help in studying the environmental problem? First, the table is useful in illustrating the interrelationships between industries. Second, the table is helpful in the study of the dynamic implications of a change in one industry. While the actual mathematical manipulations of the table are beyond the scope of this book, some intuitive use of the table will demonstrate its utility.

Assume first that consumers double their purchases of the nonpolluting good C. The expansion of output of good C will require that Industry C purchase twice as many inputs from Industries A, B, C, and the household sector. More inputs will be required from the air polluter (Industry B) and the water polluter (Industry A). As each of these industries expand to produce more inputs for C, air and water pollution increase even though C itself does not pollute.

The table can also illustrate the impact of restricting the production of a polluting good. Assume that Industry A (the water polluter) is forced to reduce output by 50 percent. This action causes a decline in sales both for Industry A and for all the industries selling inputs to Industry A. Restricting the water polluter decreases production of good A directly but also lowers the sales, purchases, production, and employment of air polluting good B and nonpolluting good C. In addition, Industry A's purchases of factor services (basically labor) from households will also decrease. Thus, the effect on employment, output, and sales of the action against Industry A spreads far beyond Industry A to all industries servicing Industry A. These secondary, or indirect, effects are often overlooked when a given action against a given industry is being contemplated. The use of an input-output table makes possible the analysis of both the direct and indirect effects of environmental policies.[10]

The Abuse of Common Property and Its Significance

Air, water, and land are essential if life is to be sustained. They are also inputs in the process of production and consumption. As indicated earlier, in many situations these inputs have been considered as free waste-discharge mechanisms. The discharges, unfortunately, accrue in the air, water, and land and threaten the life supporting

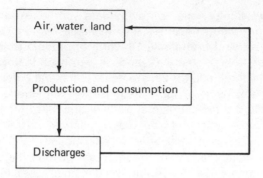

Figure 2-2

capabilities of these inputs. This accretion is shown schematically in Figure 2-2.

Prior to the Industrial Revolution, the importance of the above process was negligible. With industrial growth and population growth, however, this process becomes more significant. When only one family discharges its wastes into the Mississippi River or Lake Erie, the degree of pollution is miniscule. As other families, whole cities, and complex industries follow suit, contamination grows, and ultimately the resource is not capable of sustaining life. It has become saturated with pollutants. This problem of density of pollutants is depicted in Figure 2-3.

Initially air, water, and land are able to assimilate the discharges. As the number of users increases, the assimilation process slows and

Figure 2-3

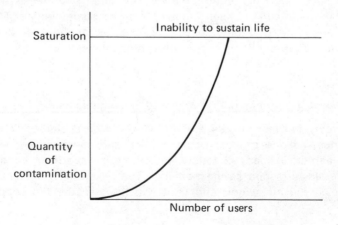

contamination increases. Ultimately, as is now the case with many of our rivers and lakes, these vital resources are unable to sustain life. Also, under certain atmospheric conditions, some cities have recorded deaths caused by air pollution. The problem is aggravated further because some discharges are not degradable and consequently are not assimilated. Mercury, DDT, and certain plastics are examples of discharges which do not break down and thus accumulate in the environment.

For too long economists have ignored air, water, land, pollution density, and industrial discharges. Recycling has been introduced only when economically feasible within the framework of the production and consumption process. Eastman Kodak Company, the largest user of silver in the United States, recovers silver from discarded motion picture films. There are many examples in which firms recover, rather than discharge, chemicals used in the production process. Certain by-products are also used rather than discharged. In each case, the value of the recovered material, in a market sense, exceeds the cost of recovery.

The topic of recycling deserves further comment, and it is useful to employ a simplified flow sheet, Figure 2-4. The production of intermediate goods and the distribution of all goods are omitted from the diagram.

First, consider the production side of the flow diagram. The discharge from the production process is divided into two parts, recoverable materials and waste. In turn, the recoverable materials are divided into two parts, those which can be recovered economically and those which cannot and are added to waste.

Technological development could reduce the amount of materials which are currently not economically recoverable. In other words, technological change could shift materials from the noneconomic waste category to the economic category of recoverable materials.

There is always waste from the production process. Again, with technological change the amount of waste can be reduced through the creation of new products from final or intermediate wastes.

A firm's investment or research and development decisions may be directed to a better use of existing resources; or, the research and investment may be directed to totally new and different products, new plants, and mergers. Expected return is an important element in a firm's decision-making process. The return measured, however, is the firm's and not society's. Society's saving from recovery may be greater than the cost of recovery, but if a firm's saving is not greater than the cost of recovery, the firm will have no incentive to undertake investment in recovery equipment.

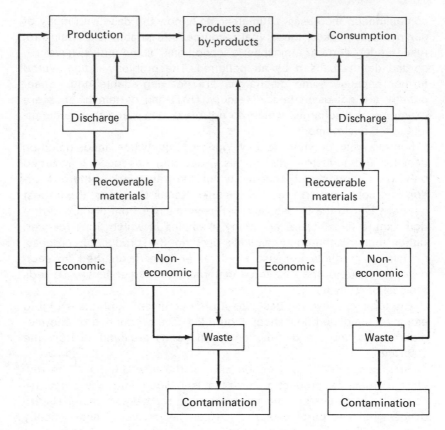

Figure 2-4

The consumption side of Figure 2-4 raises additional points. Again, the discharge can be separated into recoverable materials and waste. The recycling of recoverable materials may be economic or noneconomic, the latter being added to waste. Recycled materials may be returned to the production or consumption process. Scrap metals are recovered and reenter the production process. Other materials, such as used fenders or bumpers, enter the consumption process. Cost per unit of recovered materials compares favorably to new product and resource prices and makes recycling feasible. Sometimes materials are recycled because a firm does not incur the cost of collection; boy scout paper collection drives are an example.

Research and development can reduce the amount of noneconomically recoverable materials and waste materials, but there are additional problems. Who will conduct the necessary research and development to achieve the possible reduction? How will the necessary investment be obtained? Is it feasible to collect these materials from consumers? What incentives are there for firms to design products for recycling?

As the population grows, air, water, and land are becoming more contaminated. In order to protect these valuable resources, recycling may be required for all processes. The home or city should discharge only water, the smokestacks should discharge only air, and so on. Research and technological development must be directed toward, if not the elimination of impure discharges, the minimization of them by maximal use of recycling. Elements of the problem become worldwide and the industrialized nations bear the responsibility of taking the initiative to effect change.

It should be noted that recycling is a part of natural processes. The earth's water cycle is a closed system. Carbon dioxide is converted to oxygen by plant life. Perhaps the process of production and consumption must also become a closed system. The frontiers of the world are vanishing and the density problem is real. In the absence of population control, the only other vaguely possible solution is to create a new frontier by exporting people to outer space. In the animal kingdom, there is a geographical dispersion of the population. Each animal (or group) stakes out a territory which under existing conditions is sufficient to sustain life. Man is the exception; he congregates by creating cities and the density problem increases.

The discussion to this point has focused upon those elements which cause and contribute to the environmental problem. At the center of the problem is the fact that all costs resulting from the production of goods are not included in the prices of those goods. Some costs, such as those of effluent disposal, are shifted to society as losses of clean air and water. Correction of the environmental problem will involve enormous costs. The initial impact of the costs of environmental improvement will fall upon the polluters. The magnitude of these costs is examined in Chapter 3. The workings of the price system are such, however, that the ultimate incidence of the costs may be transferred to other economic units. The difference between the initial impact of the costs and the ultimate division of those costs will be explored in Chapter 4.

3

The Costs of Pollution Abatement

Any effort to restore and maintain the integrity of the environment imposes a cost burden on society. The magnitude and burden of these costs are of great importance. This chapter examines the sources and the estimated cost of controlling air and water pollution with particular emphasis on controlling industrial sources of pollution.

Distinguishing Air and Water Pollution

As we have seen, air and water pollution are similar in that both result from the same type of market failure. To function efficiently, the market must be able to convert the total economic cost of resource use into a private cost to the user; that is, all costs must be internalized. Thus, air and water pollution occur when the market fails to internalize the external costs associated with environmental damage. Without restraints, a freely functioning market treats air and water resources as free goods.

There are, however, several important differences between air and water pollution. In the first place, air pollution tends to be more of a local problem than water pollution. Emissions into the atmosphere are diluted as they move further away from their source. This dilution process tends to reduce the damages associated with air pollution.

Water pollution generally does not undergo a similar dilution process. Rivers tend to transport pollution from one locality to another without a substantial reduction in the pollution level. There are also important differences in man's ability to control air and water pollution. The present state of scientific knowledge allows substantially greater control over water flow and location than over meteorological occurrences. Finally, while both types of pollution are believed to have an important impact on human health, there is much more supporting evidence in the case of air pollution. The similarities and differences between air and water pollution are important considerations in developing any environmental improvement policy.[1]

Measuring Pollution

Determining the extent of the pollution problem in the United States may appear to the uninitiated to be relatively simple. There are, however, some serious obstacles to any attempt to measure pollution levels, not the least of which has been, and continues to be, the lack of accurate and comprehensive data on the current condition of the environment.

In a recent report, the Council on Environmental Quality[2] recognizes several problems: a lack of sufficient understanding of environmental phenomena to allow agreement on all elements to be measured, a lack of a comprehensive definition and evaluation of data needs, and a lack of data itself owing to inadequate technology. In spite of these problems, some data are presently available and can be used to evaluate the major sources of pollution.

Air Pollution

Air pollution results, to a large extent, from the emission of sulfur oxides, particulates, hydrocarbons, carbon monoxides, and nitrogen oxides.[3] The data contained in Table 3-1 indicate total emissions by their source during 1969. Emissions from all sources totaled 281.2 million tons in 1969, a figure which was 3.2 percent greater than the corresponding figure for 1968. Transportation, dominated by the automobile's internal combustion engine, accounts for over 50 percent of total emissions and is clearly the largest single source of emissions. The second largest air pollutant is fuel combustion in stationary sources which, in 1969, accounted for 15.8 percent of total emissions. In 1969, transportation and solid waste disposal emissions levels were slightly less than the 1968 levels. While it is too early to determine if this change represents a long-term trend, the installation of

Table 3-1 Estimated Emissions of Air Pollutants
by Weight, Nationwide, 1969
(Millions of Tons Per Year)

Source	Total	Percentage of total	Percentage of change 1968–1969
Transportation	144.4	51.4	− 1.0
Fuel combustion in stationary sources	44.3	15.8	+ 2.5
Industrial processes	39.6	14.1	+ 7.3
Solid waste disposal	11.9	4.2	− 1.0
Miscellaneous	41.0	14.6	+ 18.5
Total	281.2	100.0ᵃ	+ 3.2

ᵃ Totals may not add up to 100 percent because of rounding.
Source: Council on Environmental Quality, *Environmental Quality: The Second Annual Report on Environmental Quality* (Washington: United States Government Printing Office, August, 1971), p. 212.

emission control devices on 1968 cars and a reduction in open burning at municipal dumps have been offered as possible explanations for the lower emission levels.[4]

The data presented in Table 3-1 measure emission levels in terms of weight and as a result may be somewhat misleading. In evaluating environmental quality, primary emphasis should be placed on the effects of the various emissions and a weight measure does not reflect the fact that the effects do not necessarily correlate with the amount emitted. For example, a pound of sulfur oxides is likely to have a greater environmental effect than a pound of carbon monoxide. There are other problems with the pollution data. National figures may be misleading because they do not reflect regional differences or pollution levels which result from an uneven distribution of population and industrial activity in the United States. Even data collected by monitoring devices in a city are extremely sensitive to the location of the device. Air pollution tends to disperse as it moves away from the source of emission and two monitoring devices placed at only slightly different distances from the source often yield significantly different sets of data. For example, the Environmental Protection Agency's National Air Sampling Network (NASN) sites are generally located in the central city but the NASN data for a given city indicate significantly less air pollution than do the data collected by state and local agen-

cies in the same city. This may be because the state and local agencies are concerned with collecting data for possible legal actions and
place their monitoring devices closer to the sources of air pollution.

The Clean Air Act of 1967, with various amendments, establishes
emission control levels and air quality standards for the entire United
States. The Act requires that each state submit to the Environmental
Protection Agency (EPA) a plan for controlling emission of particulates, hydrocarbons, nitrogen oxides, and carbon monoxide. The Act
also requires the EPA to submit an annual report outlining the estimated costs of meeting the air quality standards.

Estimates of control costs for the major stationary sources of air
pollution are presented in Table 3-2. Investment costs represent total
outlays through fiscal 1977 for equipment, plus installment and start-
up costs. Annual costs are composed of operation and maintenance,
depreciation, and interest expenses. The control costs are those required to move from control levels existing in 1967 to the levels required in 1976 by the Clean Air Act. As indicated in Table 3-2, total
emissions in 1967 from the three stationary sources were 73,375,000
tons. Stationary fuel combustion involves fossil fuel combustion in
residential, commercial, industrial and steam-electric generating
plants and accounted for nearly 53 percent of total emissions in 1967.
Industrial processes are responsible for some 36 percent of total
emissions and solid waste disposal by industrial incinerators and

Table 3-2 Estimates of Emissions and Control Costs by Source

Source	1967 Total emissions[a] thousands of tons	Percentage of total	1977 Control costs[b] (000,000 dollars) Investment	Annual
Solid waste disposal	7,830	10.7	472	224
Stationary fuel combustion	38,810	52.9	5,539	2,476
Industrial processes	26,735	36.4	4,135	1,213
Total	73,375[c]	100.0	10,146	3,913

[a] Emissions covered include: particulates, sulfur oxides, carbon monoxide,
hydrocarbons, and nitrogen oxides.
[b] All cost estimates are in 1970 dollars.
[c] Emissions from mobile sources are not included.
Source: Annual Report of the Administrator of the Environmental Protection
Agency, *The Economics of Clean Air* (Washington: United States Government
Printing Office, February, 1972), p. 4-2.

dumps and open burning by municipalities and farms account for slightly more than 10 percent of total emissions.

Cost estimates reported in Table 3-2 indicate that investment outlays of $10.1 billion and annual expense of $3.9 billion are necessary if emission levels are to be made consistent with air quality levels contained in the Clean Air Act as amended in 1970. Control costs are largest in the case of stationary fuel combustion. Investment costs relative to annual costs are somewhat larger in the case of industrial processes and may simply be a reflection of the heterogeneous nature of emission control technology among the various industries grouped under the single category in Table 3-2. It should be emphasized that these figures are based upon 1967 emission levels projected to fiscal 1977 on the assumption of certain growth rates. In addition, the cost estimates in Table 3-2 represent national estimates and differ from earlier figures based on specific metropolitan areas.

Industrial Air Pollution   The preceding discussion of emission levels and control costs relates to broadly defined sectors of the economy and as such fails to indicate the extent of pollution reduction problems at the individual industry level. Estimates of the cost of controlling air pollution from industrial sources have been prepared by the Environmental Protection Agency. They cover fifteen industries and indicate the cost of bringing plants operating in 1967 and plants commencing operation during the period 1968–1976 into compliance with emission standards in 1976.

Table 3-3 lists the industries for which the Environmental Protection Agency has determined emission levels and estimated control costs. The industries differ substantially in size, ranging from petroleum refineries with 1967 shipments of $20.3 billion to the lead industry with shipments of only $130 million. The petroleum refining industry is the largest single source of emissions among the industries contained in Table 3-3. In 1967 refineries accounted for some 11.9 million tons of emissions. Other industries with large amounts of emissions include gray iron foundries and copper, iron and steel manufacturers. At the other extreme, industries such as secondary nonferrous metallurgy and aluminum and nitric acid manufacturers had relatively low emissions levels in 1967.

The final column of data presented in Table 3-3 contains a pollution intensity figure for each industry. According to one economist, a comparison of the intensity of pollution over time would provide some insight into the relationship between changes in technology and pollution levels. In addition, if there were to be a systematic movement in pollution intensity over a period of time, the failure to take account

Table 3-3   Air Pollution Levels of Various
Industrial Activities, 1967

Industry	Value of shipments (000,000 dollars)	Total emissions (000 tons)	Pollution intensity emissions per $1,000 shipments (tons)
Asphalt batching	$ 1,100	243	.22
Cement	1,200	813	.68
Grain milling	4,830	256	.05
Gray iron foundries	2,700	3,417	1.27
Iron and steel	13,300	2,310	.17
Kraft (sulfate) pulp	3,600	380	.11
Lime	240	393	1.64
Nitric acid	450	145	.32
Petroleum refineries	20,300	11,948	.59
Phosphate	980	260	.27
Primary nonferrous metallurgy:			
Aluminum	1,560	32	.02
Copper	1,120	2,823	2.52
Lead	130	219	1.68
Zinc	260	503	1.93
Secondary nonferrous metallurgy	1,480	24	.02

Source: Annual Report of the Administrator of the Environmental Protection Agency, *The Economics of Clean Air* (Washington: February, 1972), pp. 4-21, 4-22.

of it would make any projections of the need for pollution abatement facilities inaccurate.[5] The copper industry with 2.52 tons of emissions per thousand dollars of shipments has the highest intensity level. Other industries with high figures are zinc, lead, and lime. The lowest levels, only 0.02 tons, or forty pounds per thousand dollars of shipments, occur in the secondary nonferrous metallurgy and aluminum industries.

There is, then, no clear correlation between an industry's total emissions level and pollution intensity. In Table 3-4, the fifteen industries are ranked by total emissions levels as well as by pollution intensity. Petroleum refineries, ranked first in terms of absolute emissions, are ranked seventh in terms of pollution intensity. A similar situation exists for the iron and steel industry, which ranks fourth in total emission and eleventh in terms of pollution intensity. The opposite situation, industries ranking relatively higher in terms of pollution intensity, occurs among the lead, zinc, and lime industries.

The proper interpretation of the data presented in Table 3-4 is not

Table 3-4   Industry Ranking by Total Emissions
                and Pollution Intensity

| | Industry rank | |
Industry	Total emissions	Pollution intensity
Asphalt batching	11	10
Cement	5	6
Grain milling	10	13
Gray iron foundries	2	5
Iron and steel	4	11
Kraft (sulfate) pulp	8	12
Lime	7	4
Nitric acid	13	8
Petroleum refineries	1	7
Phosphate	9	9
Primary nonferrous metallurgy:		
Aluminum	14	14
Copper	3	1
Lead	12	3
Zinc	6	2
Secondary nonferrous metallurgy	15	14

Source: Computed from data in Table 3-3.

exactly clear, but it may provide some initial insight as to the causes
and, by implication, the proper solutions to air pollution problems in
specific industries. Given that technology capable of achieving zero
pollution is seldom available, emission control in an industry with a
high total emission level and a low intensity figure probably is going
to require the reduction of demand for the industry's product rather
than the adoption of new technologies. On the other hand, the development and adoption of new technologies may be called for in the
case of industries with high pollution intensity and relatively lower,
though still important, levels of total emissions. Of course, both a reduction in demand and changes in technology may be appropriate for
industries with high emission levels *and* high pollution intensity.

Industrial Air Pollution Control Costs   Identifying major sources of
industrial air pollution, in addition to being informative, serves as a
basis for estimating the costs of an emission control program. This
section presents the cost estimates developed by the EPA. The figures represent the cost of bringing each industry's emission levels
into compliance with the air quality standards set by the Clean Air

Act. Compliance must be achieved by 1976. As indicated earlier, investment costs represent cumulative outlays during 1967–1976, while annual costs indicate costs for plants in operation in 1976. The cost estimates are reported in Table 3-5.

In terms of investment outlays, the largest amount, $923 million, occurs in the aluminum industry. Other industries in which large capital expenditures are required include iron and steel, petroleum refineries, copper, and gray iron foundries. The smallest investment levels occur in the case of grain milling and lime in which, according to the EPA, investment costs are $19 million and $29 million, respectively. As a group, total investment expenditures by the fifteen industries are projected to be $3,550 million.

The EPA estimates that the highest level of annual costs will be $306 million in the iron and steel industry. Emission control efforts

Table 3-5   Estimated Control Costs for
Various Industrial Processes

Industry	Emission control costs [a] ($000,000)		Annual cost per $1000 shipments (dollars)
	Investment	Annual	
Asphalt batching	272	63	30.00
Cement	89	35	21.63
Grain milling	19	4	0.63
Gray iron foundries	348	126	33.16
Iron and steel	841	306	18.00
Kraft (sulfate) pulp	132	40	7.87
Lime	29	7	17.56
Nitric acid	37	14	n/a [b]
Petroleum refineries	378	73	n/a [b]
Phosphate	31	15	10.14
Primary nonferrous metallurgy:			
Aluminum	923	256	76.31
Copper	313	100	46.95
Lead	65	16	104.00
Zinc	41	18	55.31
Secondary nonferrous metallurgy	32	9	4.03
Total	3,550	1,082	

[a] All cost estimates represent 1970 dollars.
[b] Not applicable.
Source: Annual Report of the Administrator of the Environmental Protection Agency, *The Economics of Clean Air* (Washington: February, 1972), pp. 4-22, 4-23.

are also characterized by high operating costs in the aluminum, gray iron foundries, and copper industries.

The use of absolute figures, such as those discussed above, does not adequately reveal the impact or burden of the cost of controlling emission levels. A more complete picture can be obtained by analyzing the costs on a relative basis. Accordingly, the annual cost of emission control per thousand dollars of shipments has been computed and is reported in Table 3-5. This measure not only provides a better understanding of the cost differentials among the various industries but provides an indication of those industries in which control costs are more likely to lead to substantial price increases. The highest cost, $104 per thousand dollars of shipments, occurs in the lead industry. Yet in terms of the absolute annual costs of complying with the Clean Air Act, the lead industry has relatively low annual costs. The opposite situation occurs in the iron and steel industry, which has the highest total operating costs, $306 million, but ranks seventh in terms of costs per thousand dollars of shipments. Among other industries with high relative costs are aluminum, copper, and gray iron foundries.

The costs imposed on firms by the Clean Air Act will have an impact on prices and expenditure patterns of consumers throughout the entire economy. The costs can be expected to cause price increases of varying amounts and will lead to changes in the relative price structure between goods whose production leads to air pollution and goods whose production is relatively nonpolluting. The extent of the price increases to be expected is difficult to predict and will depend on the product's price, the elasticity of demand, the income elasticity, and the degree of competition in the specific market.

The EPA, relying on their cost estimates, has attempted to determine the likely impact of the Clean Air Act on product prices. The projected price increases likely to occur in 1977 are reported in Table 3-6. In several industries, control costs are expected to lead to substantial increases. The largest increase, 8.2 percent, is predicted for the lead industry. This is not surprising in light of the earlier evidence that the lead industry would experience annual control costs amounting to $104 per thousand dollars of shipments. In fact, with the exception of gray iron foundries, the five highest ranked industries in terms of annual costs per thousand dollars of shipments are included among the top five in terms of expected price increases. While these figures are highly tentative, it is clear that air quality programs will lead to a realignment of relative prices. In terms of the impact on the aggregate price level, the EPA predicts an overall increase of only 0.7 percent in 1977, with nearly all of the increase

Table 3-6 Estimated 1977 Price Increase Due to
Emission Control Costs by Industry

Industry	Estimated price increase (%)
Asphalt	3.0
Cement	2.2
Grain milling	0.1
Gray iron foundries	2.6
Iron and steel	1.2
Kraft (sulfate) pulp	0.7
Lime	1.8
Nitric acid	0.0
Petroleum refineries	0.0
Phosphate	0.5
Primary nonferrous metallurgy:	
Aluminum	7.0
Copper	5.7
Lead	8.2
Zinc	7.1
Secondary nonferrous metallurgy	0.4

Source: Annual Report of the Administrator of the Environmental Protection Agency, *The Economics of Clean Air,* p. 5-6.

resulting from high prices for motor vehicles and electricity. Although
these predictions are only approximations of the actual results, it is
clear that the impact of controlling air pollution from industrial
sources is not likely to lead to a radical restructuring of the composition of GNP or expenditure patterns.

Water Pollution

An economic analysis of water pollution is inhibited by the same
sorts of problems as the analysis of air pollution: lack of a comprehensive definition of water pollution; incomplete quantification of the
volume of wastes by industrial sources; incomplete knowledge of the
impact of technological change in various industries on the volume of
wastes discharged; and the lack of comprehensive cost estimates for
industrial water pollution control.[6] These deficiencies become crucial
when the analysis moves from a simple identification of materials discharged to bodies of water to an actual measurement of the extent of
the problem.

Certain institutional factors also impede an analysis of the economics of water pollution. For example, the *Census of Manufactures'*
data concerning water use by manufacturing industries is treated as

confidential by the Bureau of the Census. Data indicating water use quantities obviously are a crucial input for accurate analysis of industrial pollution; such information is especially important for assessing water pollution problems at regional levels. In industries composed of only a few firms, publication of water use data might allow the identification of the amount of water used by a particular firm or plant. The rationale for treating the amount of water used as proprietary information is difficult to understand, inasmuch as the need for such data has been clearly established.

Measuring Water Quality   Water quality levels are generally defined in terms of the impact of waste discharges on a five day biochemical oxygen demand, commonly referred to as BOD. BOD represents the quantity of oxygen consumed in a fixed period of time and at a constant temperature by the biological processes involved in the stabilization of organic matter.[7] A body of water with a high BOD level is likely to have lower concentrations of dissolved oxygen, a significant chemical oxygen demand, and higher than normal bacteria levels.[8] Consequently, the higher the BOD level, the lower the water quality, and vice versa.

In spite of its general use as an indicator of water quality, the BOD level is not suitable in all cases. For instance, water pollution resulting from discharges of mercury, pesticides, and toxic materials is not reflected in BOD measures.

Aggregate BOD Production   The EPA has attempted to estimate gross BOD production for certain years during the period 1957–1968. Household production of BOD is estimated by reference to municipal waste inventories, which are generally reliable guides to the oxygen demand created by public wastes.[9] Estimation techniques employed in the case of manufacturing are much less precise and yield estimates that are only gross approximations of the true values.[10] Manufacturing BOD levels are estimated by comparing a 1964 ratio of waste production to output with Federal Reserve Board indices of physical output for 1957 and 1968. There are several deficiencies in this technique, but the most serious is perhaps the implicit assumption that the waste/output ratio is constant over the period 1957–68. In effect, it is assumed that changes in technology are neutral in their impact on water production.[11] The estimates, as developed by the EPA, are presented in Table 3-7.

The figures in Table 3-7 indicate that total BOD production increased from 20,790 million pounds in 1957 to 38,170 million pounds

Table 3-7   Gross Production of BOD, 1957–1968
            (Millions of Pounds of BOD)

Source	1957	1964	1968	Increase 1957–1964	Increase 1964–1968
Total manufacturing	15,090	22,460	29,670	7,370	7,220
Sewered population	5,700	7,600	8,500	2,100	900
Total	20,790	30,060	38,170	9,470	8,120
Annual rate				5.4%	6.2%
Reduced by treatment	8,090	14,090	24,610	6,000	10,520
Annual rate				8.2%	15.0%
Discharged	12,700	15,970	13,560	3,270	− 2410
Annual rate				5.9%	− 4.2%
Treatment efficiency	39%	47%	64%	21.0%	36.0%
Ratio of industrial to domestic BOD	2.6:1	2.9:1	3.5:1	3.5:1	8.0:1

Source: Increases computed from information in Environmental Protection Agency, *The Cost of Clean Water* (Washington: United States Government Printing Office, March, 1971), Vol. II, *Cost Effectiveness and Clean Water*, p. 29.

in 1968. Manufacturing activity produces much greater levels of BOD than do domestic or household sources, though this may not be the case in certain regions of the United States. For instance, on the Pacific coast and in the Plains states, agriculture is the major source of water pollution. In the Central states, municipal wastes are the major source.[12] It is not surprising that manufacturing activity also accounts for most of the increase in BOD production during the period 1957–1968. It is important to realize, however, that BOD production is not identical with pollution level. In terms of impact on water quality the important variable is BOD discharge not BOD production. The ratio of industrial to domestic BOD production has been consistently increasing since 1957 and was 3.5 to 1.0 in 1968.

The data contained in Table 3-7 also illustrate the increasing effectiveness of treatment facilities. While gross production of BOD continued to expand during the period 1957–1968, the estimated level of BOD discharge in 1968 was actually less than the 1964 level and was only slightly larger than the 1957 level. During the period 1964–1968, BOD discharge decreased by 2,410 million pounds or 4.2 percent. It is tempting to conclude that the water pollution problem has been at least stabilized. However, the Council on Environmental Quality cautions against such a conclusion and points out that in spite of the apparent reduction in BOD discharge levels, the general quality of the nation's water supply continues to decline.[13]

Characteristics of Water Use and Pollution by Industry The preceding discussion indicates that industrial sources are the major source of BOD production in the United States. The demand for treatment facilities results largely from increased BOD output by industry and a marked increase in the tendency of industry to discharge wastes into municipal treatment plants.

The relationship between increased industrial discharge into public treatment facilities and the demand for municipal treatment plants is more than simply quantitative. In addition to volume, waste discharges by industry have two characteristics distinguishing them from domestic or household discharges. Industrial loadings tend to have significant volume fluctuations. Domestic discharges fluctuate on an hourly basis with peak flows occurring during morning and evening hours, but industrial loadings, especially those from industries with seasonal changes in production levels, often have much greater fluctuations. In 1964 seasonal food processing industries were estimated to have accounted for nearly 25 percent of total industrial discharge to public sewers.[14] Given that treatment plant capacity is determined by peak period demand rather than average annual demand, the industrial loadings into public treatment plants requires the construction of much larger and more costly plants. There is, however, substantial evidence to indicate the existence of significant scale economies in these plants.[15] Industrial loadings or discharges, compared to domestic flows, also tend to have a higher concentration of waste materials, which, depending on the particular materials, may increase or decrease treatment costs. The Federal Water Pollution Control Administration estimates that industrial wastes treated in public plants account for up to 63 percent of total gross volume of oxygen demanding materials.[16] In general, the treatment of both domestic and industrial flows in the same plant is likely to increase construction and operating costs.

Water Use in Manufacturing The Bureau of the Census has, since 1953, published a report entitled "Water Use in Manufacturing" as part of the *Census of Manufactures.*[17] The report presents data on water intake, use, and discharge for individual industries as defined by the Standard Industrial Classification Code. The data are the closest approximation to a national inventory of industrial waste sources and is obviously of great value. The data suffer from several weaknesses in addition to the Census Bureau's decision to treat the information as proprietary and therefore subject to disclosure rules. The disclosure rule is applied in any case where the release of industry information would disclose operating characteristics of any

Table 3-8 Gross Water Use and Value Added by Manufacturing Group

Industry group	Value added[a] 1967 Millions dollars	% Total	Gross water use, incl. recirculation 1968 (bills. gals)	% Total	Main purpose of water intake
Food and food products	12,067	9.6	1,346	3.8	Cooling and condensing except air conditioning
Textile mill products	3,732	3.0	328	0.9	Processing
Paper and allied products	4,968	4.0	6,522	18.3	Processing
Chemicals and allied products	16,131	12.9	9,416	26.4	Cooling and condensing except air conditioning
Petroleum and coal products	4,612	3.7	7,290	20.4	Cooling and condensing except air conditioning
Rubber and plastics	3,352	2.7	269	0.8	Cooling and condensing except air conditioning
Primary metals	14,798	11.8	7,780	21.8	Cooling and condensing except air conditioning
Machinery, except electrical	10,898	8.7	338	0.9	Steam electric power generation
Transportation equipment	21,401	17.1	911	2.6	Boiler feed, sanitary service, and other
Other	33,459	26.7	1,501	4.2	
All manufacturing	125,417	100.0	35,701	100.0	Cooling and condensing except air conditioning

Source: United States Bureau of the Census, *Census of Manufactures, 1967, Water Use in Manufacturing* (Washington: United States Government Printing Office, MC67(1)-7, 1971), pp. 7-5, 7-16, 7-17, 7-23 through 7-28.
[a] Establishments reporting water consumption of twenty million gallons or more.

individual firm. The data appear only at five year intervals and with a long lag. Furthermore, the data are based upon a sample of only large water users. Establishments using twenty million gallons or more of water were included in the 1968 sample. These firms account for 44 percent of total manufacturing employment and for an estimated 97 percent of water withdrawn for manufacturing purposes.

The data contained in Table 3-8 indicate value added and gross water use for broadly defined manufacturing groups. Gross water use, as defined by the Bureau of the Census, is the estimated equivalent water volume that would have been necessary if no water had been recirculated. Consequently, if a firm recirculates some of the original water intake, gross water use will exceed total water intake. Value added is defined as the difference between the value of an industry's shipments and the total cost of materials used.

The most striking impression from Table 3-8 is the highly uneven distribution of water use among the various manufacturing groups. The five largest users — chemicals, primary metals, petroleum and coal products, paper and allied products, and food — account for over 90 percent of total water use by all manufacturing. At the other extreme, textiles, rubber, and machinery are relatively small water users with each accounting for less than 1 percent of the total.

Among the larger water users, water use tends to be disproportionately large compared to the industry's share of value added in manufacturing. For instance, the chemical group accounts for 26 percent of total water use but only 13 percent of manufacturing value added. The petroleum industry accounts for 20.4 and 3.7 percent of water use and value added, respectively. A similar situation exists in the paper industry. The opposite situation, a disproportionately small share of water use, occurs in the case of the transportation and machinery groups. It should be understood that the industry categories listed in Table 3-8 are highly aggregated and do not precisely correspond to the economic concept of an industry. Consequently, the figures may conceal very important differences in water use at the more narrowly defined industry level. The disparity between value added and water use shares, however, does indicate that industrial water use is not simply a function of output levels.

Efficiency of Water Use — The Recirculation Index   The efficiency of water use in manufacturing can be examined in part by determining the extent to which industries reuse the original water intake. This aspect of water use can be examined by computing an index of water recirculation, which is the ratio of gross water use to total water intake. A higher ratio indicates a more intense use of the original water intake and can be interpreted as indicating a more efficient use of water. These indices, computed for a cross section of manufacturing groups, provide some insight into the question of whether significant differences exist in the efficiency of water use among the various groups.

Recirculation indices computed for 1959, 1964, and 1968 are presented in Table 3-9. In 1959, manufacturing firms recirculated and reused an average of 216 gallons of water for each 100 gallons of original water intake. The value of the index fell slightly in 1964 but increased to a value of 231 per hundred by 1968. There is substantial variation in the value of the index among the various manufacturing groups. The highest value, 508, occurs in the petroleum and coal products group. Other industries in which the recirculation index exceeds the average for all manufacturing firms are transportation equipment, paper, and paper products. Relatively low values characterize water use efficiency in the primary metals, food, and machinery groups.

In several cases there has been a marked trend toward a more efficient use of the original water intake. Industries with significant increases in the recirculation index include textiles, chemicals, petroleum and coal products, and transportation equipment. The recirculation index calculated for the food group indicates a substantial reduction in water use efficiency during the period 1959–1968. A

Table 3-9 Ratio of Gross Water Use to Total Water Intake by Industry Group 1959–1968

	1959	1964	1968
Food and food processing	208	157	166
Textile mill products	135	182	213
Paper and allied products	312	266	290
Chemicals	161	198	210
Petroleum and coal products	438	441	508
Rubber and plastics	172	199	199
Primary metals	153	146	155
Machinery, except electrical	147	173	179
Transportation equipment	201	249	291
All manufacturing	216	213	231

Source: United States Bureau of the Census, *Census of Manufactures, 1967, Water Use in Manufacturing* (Washington: United States Government Printing Office, MC67(1)-7, 1967), pp. 7-16, 7-17.

similar, although much smaller, decrease occurred in the paper and paper products group during the same period.

The existence of a trend toward increased efficiency is impressive, but in three of the five largest water using groups the value of the recirculation index was less than the average value for all manufacturing. This is the case for the food, chemical, and primary metals manufacturing groups, suggesting that some of the largest water users are not even matching the average improvements in water use efficiency in the manufacturing sector. A more efficient use of water, however, does not necessarily imply a reduction in the volume of waste materials discharged into water bodies.

Gross BOD Production by Manufacturing Process Estimates of gross BOD production for various manufacturing groups are presented in Table 3-10. As noted previously, the 1964 figures are based upon estimates of BOD levels and the 1957 and 1968 data are arrived at by applying the 1964 output-BOD ratio to 1957 and 1968 output levels. However serious the deficiencies involved in assuming a constant output-BOD ratio might be, the resulting figures identify the relative importance of each group in terms of BOD production.

The contribution of each manufacturing group to total BOD production by manufacturing activity is indicated in Table 3-10. In 1968, total BOD output was 29,670 million pounds and the chemical and paper groups accounted for 47.9 and 26.3 percent of the total respectively. The five largest water using groups, identified in Table 3-10 as chemicals, primary metals, petroleum, paper, and food, are, according to the estimates in Table 3-10, responsible for nearly 94 percent of manufacturing BOD levels in 1968. Of this group, however, petroleum and metals account for less than 4 percent of total BOD. Clearly, the major industrial sources of water pollution, measured in terms of BOD output, are the chemicals, paper, and food groups.

The increase in BOD output from each manufacturing source is also indicated in Table 3-10. Since a constant output-BOD ratio was assumed during the period 1957–1968, movements in the percentage of increase in BOD output attributable to each group are simply a reflection of the change in each group's production level during the periods, 1957–1964 and 1964–1968. In both periods, chemicals, a fast growing industry, accounted for substantially more than 50 percent of the increase in BOD output.

The evidence on water use and BOD output in manufacturing activities strongly indicates that water pollution problems are concen-

Table 3-10   Estimated Gross Production of BOD
by Manufacturing Operations: 1957–1968
(Millions of Pounds of BOD)

Industry group	Percentage of total 1957	1964	1968	Increase in BOD production 1957–1964 % of total	1964–1968 % of total
Food	22.5	19.1	15.6	12.2	4.2
Textile	4.4	4.0	3.7	3.1	2.9
Paper	28.5	26.3	26.3	21.7	26.3
Chemicals	36.4	43.2	47.9	57.0	62.3
Petroleum and coal products	2.7	2.2	1.9	1.2	0.7
Rubber and plastics	0.1	0.2	0.2	0.3	0.3
Primary metals	2.3	2.1	1.9	1.8	1.0
Machinery	0.7	0.6	0.7	0.4	0.7
Transportation equipment	0.3	0.5	0.5	0.9	0.6
All other	2.0	1.7	1.6	1.2	1.2
Total[a]	100.0	100.0	100.0	100.0	100.0
Total manufacturing BOD	15,090	22,460	29,670	7,370	7,220

[a] May not add to 100 due to rounding.
Source: Environmental Protection Agency, *The Cost of Clean Water* (Washington: United States Government Printing Office, March, 1971), Vol. II, p. 29.

trated in a few industrial groups, namely chemicals, paper, and food. This does not rule out the possibility that significant pollution problems may occur at the local level from industries which account for only small shares of national water use and pollution levels.

Industrial Water Pollution Control Costs   Industrial waste treatment costs estimated by the EPA, while related to volume of water use and discharge volumes, are also affected by residuals characteristics, waste segregation opportunities, and available technology. In addition, cost estimates for specific industries are heavily influenced by the age distribution and location of plants.

   The cost estimates reported by the EPA in 1972 represent not only an updating of past data, but a significant improvement in methodology.[18] As in the past, cost estimates are based on the volume of waste discharges and the characteristics of the waterborne discharges of manufacturing processes in specific industries, combined with information indicating flow to cost relationships.

Methodological improvements result because the 1972 estimates represent a more comprehensive coverage of industrial treatment costs. In the past, estimates were based upon water use data obtained from the Census publication entitled *Water Use in Manufacturing*. The major weakness of this approach is that Census compiles water use data only for those establishments with annual water intake of twenty million gallons or more. The EPA has constructed an evaluation model that expands coverage to include plants with annual intake volume of ten million gallons or more per year. In aggregate terms, this increases the number of establishments covered by some 50 percent, although in the case of food processing, wood products, and leather the increase is close to 100 percent.[19]

The 1972 procedure represents an improvement for a second reason. In determining the pollution potential and treatment costs, the purpose of water use is as important as the amount of water used. For instance, the pollution potential of process water is greater than the pollution potential of water used for cooling. As a result, the distribution of water use by purpose has now been incorporated into the cost estimates.

The industrial cost model used to generate cost estimates contains several assumptions concerning the manner in which firms respond to current state and Federal water quality standards. The net effect of the assumptions is to cause the model to yield the highest possible costs to be incurred in complying with water quality standards. Actual costs, therefore, are likely to be somewhat less than the estimates. Cost savings are possible by substituting capital for labor and with substitution between capital and land in the treatment process. These actions can yield substantial savings, but such adjustments are not part of the model used to generate the cost estimates.

The results are reported in Table 3-11. Estimates represent the costs of complying with 1971 water quality standards and are expressed in terms of 1967 dollars. The figures include the replacement value of existing facilities and the value of treatment services provided by public agencies.

For the entire manufacturing sector, capital costs of some $9.9 billion would be required to achieve compliance with current standards. Capital outlays are distributed among the various industrial groups

Table 3-11 Maximum Industrial Waste Treatment Costs
(1968 Flow Conditions)

| Industry | Investment | Replacement[a] | Annual cost | | | Total |
			Interest[b]	Operation		
Food and food products	$ 997.5	$ 49.9	$ 76.8	$ 57.6		$ 184.3
Textiles	251.4	12.6	19.4	11.4		43.4
Lumber and wood products	186.1	9.3	14.3	10.1		33.7
Paper and allied products	1550.5	77.3	119.4	112.3		309.0
Chemical and allied products	2436.8	121.8	187.6	123.9		433.3
Petroleum and coal products	1096.1	54.8	84.4	48.4		187.6
Rubber and plastics	96.1	4.8	7.4	6.1		18.3
Leather	86.8	4.3	6.7	4.3		15.3
Stone, clay, glass	182.3	9.1	14.0	21.3		44.6
Primary metals	1620.5	81.0	124.8	147.3		353.1
Fabricated metal products	1124.1	6.2	9.6	12.6		28.4
Machinery	100.1	5.0	7.7	10.7		23.4
Electrical equipment	129.5	6.5	10.0	14.1		30.6
Transportation equipment	122.7	6.2	9.4	15.9		31.5
All manufacturing	9852.0	448.3	690.4	606.3		

[a] A 20 year average life of equipment is assumed.
[b] Based on a 7.7 percent rate of interest.
Source: Environmental Protection Agency, *The Economics of Clean Water* (Washington: United States Government Printing Office, 1972), Vol. I, p. 63.

very unevenly, but in a way that roughly reflects water use and output levels. The largest capital costs occur in the chemicals and primary metals industries, whose costs would be $2.4 and $1.6 billion respectively. The five largest water users — chemicals, primary metals, petroleum products, paper, and food — in addition to accounting for some 90 percent of gross water use and 42 percent of manufacturing value added in 1967, account for slightly more than 78 percent of total capital expenditures.

Public concern with pollution control costs generally focuses upon capital requirements. This is natural in light of the size of the initial outlays, but over the useful life of the equipment annual costs become much more important. In fact, initial capital costs represent only about 25 percent of the total cost of treating industrial waterborne wastes. Annual costs, reported in Table 3-11 include depreciation, interest expenses, and operating and maintenance costs. For the manufacturing sector as a whole, interest expenses represent 39.7 percent, operating expenses 34.5 percent, and replacement costs 25.8 percent of annual operating costs. In the case of individual industries, the same general pattern exists: interest costs represent the largest source of annual costs followed by operating and replacement costs.

It should be emphasized again that the cost figures presented in Table 3-11 may be biased upward. The cost model tends to generate costs associated with capital intensive treatment methods and in reality firms are likely to be able to substitute labor for capital and obtain cost savings. Such a decision obviously depends upon the movement of relative prices of capital and labor. In short, pollution control costs are controllable, the extent of control being heavily dependent on the skills of management. As the EPA notes, however, the cost burdens are likely to fall most heavily upon antiquated plants in a given industry.

Relative Cost Burden   The cost data presented in Table 3-11, while not to be interpreted as definitive, provide some initial insight into the distribution of costs among manufacturing groups, but they do not provide any insight into the extent to which control costs represent a burden among the industries. The ultimate question, perhaps, concerns the extent to which pollution control costs are to be translated into higher product prices.

Some insight into relative cost burdens can be obtained on the basis of waste treatment cost estimates published by McGraw-Hill and Company. The figures are obtained from a survey of firms as to past and projected outlays for waste treatment facilities. The McGraw-Hill figures are not comparable with the cost estimates generated by EPA.

On the basis of industry supplied data, the cost of bringing United States manufacturing industries into full compliance with water quality standards by 1976 is predicted to require outlays of ten to twenty-five billion dollars between 1968 and 1976.[20] The exact amount depends mainly on the type of compliance strategy adopted by individual firms, for example, the distribution of treatment between private and public facilities.

Several institutional factors suggest that further increases in the proportion of industrial discharge being treated by public facilities are not likely.[21] In addition, the EPA has concluded that cooperative treatment arrangements among the large water users are becoming less attractive.[22]

Some indication of the relative burden of pollution control costs and the extent to which upward pressures on prices are generated can be obtained by comparing incremental treatment costs to value added for each industry. Incremental costs, as reported in Table 3-12, represent the difference between the value of treatment facilities available in 1968 and the amount necessary for full compliance with water quality standards. The incremental costs are compared to each industry's value added in 1968 and should provide some indication of possible cost increases resulting from treatment costs.

In terms of the entire manufacturing sector, the incremental costs required to meet full compliance in 1976 represent only 0.2 percent of total manufacturing value added. The $514.8 million expenditure, when considered in terms of the total cost of resources used in manufacturing, looks astonishingly small. At the industry level, incremental costs range from highs of 1.0 and 0.8 percent in paper and primary metals to lows of 0.03 and 0.01 percent in electrical equipment and transportation equipment.

On the basis of the figures in Table 3-12, upward pressures on prices arising from the costs of industry compliance with water quality goals should not, in general, be great but will be strongest in the case of paper and primary metals. The exact increase can be estimated with any reliability only by using an input-output technique.

Industrial Waste Treatment   Industrial waste treatment of water-borne wastes can be accomplished by several means including the

Table 3-12 Incremental Waste Treatment Costs
Related to Value Added 1968

Industry	Increase cost for full compliance (000,000 dollars)	Incremental value added (percent)
Food and food products	82.1	0.3
Textiles	20.9	0.2
Lumber and wood products	16.9	0.3
Paper and allied products	100.4	1.0
Chemical and allied products	47.0	0.2
Petroleum and coal products	23.9	0.1
Rubber and plastics	11.5	0.2
Leather	8.9	0.3
Stone, clay, glass	30.0	0.3
Primary metals	172.2	0.8
Fabricated metal products	25.7	0.1
Machinery	8.6	0.03
Electrical equipment	8.4	0.03
Transportation equipment	2.3	0.01
All manufacturing	514.8	0.2

Source: Environmental Protection Agency, *The Economics of Clean Water*
(Washington: United States Government Printing Office, 1972), Vol. I, p. 98.

construction of waste treatment facilities before discharge, the discharge of wastes to land by surface irrigation or well injection, the discharge of wastes to sewers and eventual treatment by municipal facilities, and changes in manufacturing processes. In recent years, the growth of industrial output has exceeded the growth of industrial discharges. Excluding Alaska and Hawaii, during 1964 and 1968 value added, in constant dollars, expanded at an annual rate of 4.8 percent while the volume of discharge grew at a rate of 2.1 percent. This represents a change from the period 1959–1964, during which value added and discharge volume grew at annual rates of 2.2 and 2.7 percent respectively.

Information presented in Table 3-13 indicates the percentage of industrial discharge receiving treatment and the annual rate of growth in treatment for the various industrial groupings. The highest percentage of treatment occurs in the petroleum and coal groups where some 75 percent of waste water discharge was treated in 1968. The lowest percentage, 5.4 percent, is associated with rubber production. During the period 1959–1968, all of the industries, with the exception

Table 3-13 Percentage of Industrial Wastewater Receiving Treatment and Growth in Treatment by Industry Groups, 1959–1968

Industry group	Percentage of industrial wastewater discharge treated			Annual rate of growth of treated discharge		
	1959	1964	1968	1959–1968	1959–1964	1964–1968
Food and kindred products	13.0	22.9	24.6	10.7	16.4	4.0
Textile mill products	14.2	25.9	39.7	13.7	15.5	11.5
Lumber	24.6	27.6	20.4	– 5.3	1.9	–13.5
Paper	41.8	36.4	44.0	2.1	–1.0	6.7
Chemicals	16.3	16.0	16.1	3.4	3.4	3.4
Petroleum and coal	54.5	76.4	75.4	3.8	8.9	– 1.8
Rubber	3.4	7.8	5.4	6.4	17.6	– 6.3
Leather	16.7	63.6	66.7	19.6	28.5	9.3
Stone, clay and glass	4.2	18.8	16.5	14.1	30.0	– 3.2
Primary metals	15.1	26.9	30.8	11.5	16.7	5.4
Fabricated metals	7.3	12.0	13.8	13.0	14.9	10.7
Machinery	18.8	8.0	13.8	– 2.3	–17.4	20.0
Electrical equipment	8.0	17.0	23.7	16.7	16.5	16.9
Transportation equipment	9.6	10.3	7.8	.5	1.8	– 1.1

Source: Environmental Protection Agency, *The Economics of Clean Water* (Washington: United States Government Printing Office, 1972), Vol. I, p. 27.

of lumber and machinery, displayed increases in the percentage of discharge being treated.

It should be emphasized that the increased amount of waste water treatment, as indicated by the data in Table 3-13, does not necessarily mean a reduction in the amount of industrial pollutants eventually finding their way to bodies of water. This interpretation is prohibited because the data does not include discharge volumes of small — less than twenty million gallons per year — water users; since there is no precise definition of water treatment, some treatment activities may not represent waste reducing activities; and there is no data to determine the degree of treatment received before discharge.

The estimated costs of controlling air and water pollution, then, while large in absolute terms, do not generally impose excessive burdens when pollution control costs are viewed in the context of the total cost of resource use in manufacturing. The evidence indicates, however, that the cost burden of industrial pollution control is unevenly distributed among industries and within a given industry, the heaviest burdens falling on older plants. Some price increases are likely to occur as a result of pollution control costs but they will probably be minimal.

4

The Imposition and Incidence of Abatement Costs

Analysis of the cost of pollution abatement is only the first step in improving the environment. The next step is to determine how society can impose the costs of environmental improvement upon the polluter. At the same time, although the polluter bears the initial impact of environmental costs, we must ask whether polluters will be able to shift those costs to other economic units so that the ultimate incidence, or burden, of the costs will be different from the initial impact.

Imposing Abatement Costs

Abatement costs can be imposed in a variety of ways, but four basic policy alternatives stand out: regulation, user charges, effluent charges, and subsidies.

Regulation Regulation requires the establishment and enforcement of quality standards or use regulations for air, water, and land. Regulations may be established either by legislation or by a regulatory agency. The enforcement powers provided by enabling legislation are usually vested in a governmental agency, commission, or board.

Environmental regulation may take a number of forms. Discharge of dangerous substances can be prohibited. Specific methods for treating and specific procedures for handling wastes can be mandated. The quantity of discharge can be limited, either for a given firm or for a group of firms each of which discharges wastes into a single receptor. Finally, regulations may be specified to maintain the quality of a given waste receptor at a given level.

Regardless of the form of the regulations, the standard-setting and enforcement processes are critical to the success of the program. Neither strictly enforced poor regulations nor poorly enforced good regulations will lead to improvement of the quality of the environment.

If regulations are to be effective, firms must reduce or eliminate pollution-producing wastes. The reduction of wastes requires expenditures for capital goods and for operating costs by the polluters. Thus, the initial impact falls upon the polluter. A public subsidy program, however, could transfer part or all of the polluter's expenses to the taxpayer. Alternatively, the polluter may be able to shift part or all of the costs to his customers.

Of critical importance in the design of environmental regulations is the determination of the geographical extent of the rules. Regulations made on a state-by-state basis change the cost of production between states and may encourage firms to move plants from states with relatively stringent controls to states with weaker controls or poorer enforcement procedures. Regulations imposed on a national basis may create economic incentives for firms to move production to other nations or may make foreign produced goods less expensive than domestically produced goods.

User Charges   A second alternative involves the use of centralized treatment facilities by several public and private polluters. This type of collective or regional approach can be used for water and land disposal but is obviously not feasible for air pollution problems.

In its most common form, the user charge approach would involve government financing of the facility with user charges being set at a level sufficient to amortize the costs of construction and pay the normal operating costs. Use of the central facility can either be optional with each polluter (so that each would have an opportunity to find a lower cost alternative treatment process) or compulsory for all polluters.

For water treatment, the central facility could treat the outflows of both industry and municipalities. If there are economies of scale in the treatment of water, the user charge approach would represent a method of lowering the cost of improving water quality and could present the means for achieving more effective treatment of water.

Refuse disposal is another pollution problem which can be approached on the user charge basis. Incinerators or sanitary land fill dumps for geographic regions, financed by user charges, may represent the most economical method of dealing with the mounting piles of waste generated by an affluent society.

While the basic concept of user charges implies a charge sufficient to amortize construction and cover operating costs, supplementary use of the subsidy approach could be made. In fact, in most cases there would be subsidization of the project by a governmental unit, because the state or local government could raise capital at a lower cost than could any business firm. The costs imposed on the business users of the treatment facilities would be an addition to their variable costs of production. The business user, however, would be able to avoid the costs of raising capital for his own treatment facility and would also save costs to the extent that economies of scale were realized by the central facility.

Effluent Charges   The effluent charge approach establishes prices for the discharge of wastes into the environment. The imposition of the charge compensates the public for the use of the environment and naturally serves as a deterrent to pollution. Given an effluent charge, some polluters will find that the effluent charge is lower than the cost of treating their wastes and will continue to discharge. Other polluters will find that the lowest cost approach will be to reduce discharges and avoid the effluent charge.

The appropriate level of the effluent charge would depend on the degree to which society desired to reduce discharges into the environment, the assimilative capacity of the waste receptor, and the type of discharge. All of these elements present substantial measurement problems.

The effluent charge approach, like the other approaches, requires some administrative control and enforcement machinery. The greatest administrative problem is the establishment of a charge sufficient both to compensate the public for the continued use losses and to encourage the appropriate degree of discharge reduction.

Subsidies   Public assumption of the costs of environmental improvement through the existing tax mechanism is a possible, though not very popular, approach to the problem. The argument can be made that all citizens are collectively responsible for the environmental problem and that the simplest, quickest, and most direct solution would be to increase taxes and use governmental borrowing power to pay for the costs of eliminating all public and private sources of environmental damage.

In this case, unlike the other cases, the impact of the costs of environmental improvement would fall not on the specific polluters but on the general taxpayer. Given that everyone is both a taxpayer and a polluter (either directly or by purchasing products manufactured under polluting conditions), there is some appeal to this approach. Of course, each person's share of the taxes might not be equal to his share of the pollution.

Equally as important, taxpayers will resist subsidizing the costs of abatement because they believe that they have already subsidized the polluter by allowing past discharges. The use of the river has not cost the firm anything but has imposed costs upon the citizen-taxpayer in the form of the loss of clean water uses of the river. Having subsidized the firm once by sacrificing clean water uses of the river, the taxpayer is unlikely to subsidize the polluting firm a second time to pay for abatement.

The Incidence of Abatement Costs

The techniques outlined in the previous section indicate the methods by which abatement costs may be imposed on those responsible for pollution. The concern was only with the initial impact. The further question is the incidence of these costs. More specifically, will these costs be passed on to others by the polluter?

Those costs which are imposed upon governmental units for sewage treatment and refuse disposal systems clearly will be shifted to the taxpayer in the form of either user charges or general taxes. In the private sector of the economy, prices, costs, and output levels will be changed by the imposition of these new costs. The analysis of the incidence of abatement costs begins with the assumption of perfect competition and progresses to more difficult real world conditions.

Adjustments Under Perfect Competition If perfectly competitive conditions exist in all markets, the environmental problem is attributable to externalities and the lack of definition of property rights. Assume, for example, that all firms are ordered to cease polluting and that only additions to fixed costs are required for perfect treatment of all wastes.

Before the imposition of the new costs, the firm's and the industry's positions are as shown in Figure 4-1. The requirement to improve the environment causes an upward shift in the firm's average

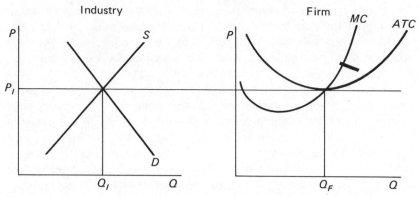

Figure 4-1

total cost curve and results in an economic loss to all firms. As a consequence, some firms will leave the industry and supply will decrease. After all adjustments are made, the firm's and industry's positions will be as illustrated in Figure 4-2.

Note that industry output has decreased but that the output of each of the remaining firms has increased. The price of the product has also increased. With lower output, some of the labor and capital previously employed in this industry has moved to other industries. Since perfect mobility of the factors of production is assumed, the adjustment is frictionless and full employment is maintained.

Figure 4-2

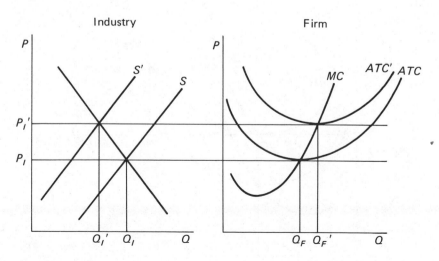

The price of the product being produced by this industry would now reflect the full cost of production; the allocation of resources would now be more nearly perfect. The higher price of the formerly polluting good discourages its use and leads to the use of other substitute goods.

The case in Figures 4-1 and 4-2 assumed that all the costs of environmental protection were fixed. At the other extreme, abatement costs could all be variable costs. Assume that all costs are variable and are a constant dollar amount per unit of output. The following equations, where TC = total cost, TFC = total fixed cost, TVC = total variable cost, N = number of units of output, and C = abatement cost per unit of output, show the before and after abatement cost relationships:

$$\text{Before: } TC = TFC + TVC$$
$$\text{After: } \quad TC = TFC + TVC + NC$$

Under these conditions, the marginal cost, average total cost, and average variable cost curves of the firm shift upwards by the amount of C. The result is shown in Figure 4-3.

The industry adjustment would involve an exodus of firms, a decrease in supply, and an increase in price. The new equilibrium industry price would equal the new marginal cost curve (MC) for the firm at the same level of output. Again, maintaining the assumption of

Figure 4-3

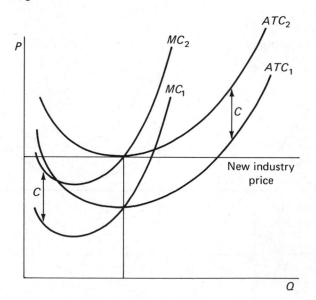

perfect mobility, resources would be transferred to other industries and resource allocation would be improved.

Thus, in the perfect competition case, the addition of the costs of environmental improvement increases price by the full amount of the increase in costs. The firms were not earning greater than normal profits in the beginning and would not be earning greater than normal profits at the end. The maintenance of normal profits would require that the added costs be passed on to the purchasers of the product. Firms would leave the industry until the supply and demand for the product determined a price at which the remaining firms could earn a normal profit.

The size of the reduction in the industry's output (or the number of firms which must leave the industry) would be related to the elasticity of demand for the industry's product. If the demand for the product in Figure 4-3 had been more elastic, a larger decrease in supply would be required to restore a normal profit level to the typical firm. Furthermore, this example assumes that an equal amount of cost increase would be imposed upon all firms in the industry. This situation would not apply if only a few states imposed environmental costs. If only some firms were to be forced to bear these costs, they would have earned less than normal profits and would have left the industry, or, given the assumption of mobility, would have moved to the states not imposing the environmental costs. A normal profit equilibrium would be reestablished, but the locational distribution of the firms would have been changed in the process.

Market Imperfections   Competition, however, is not perfect. Where monopolistic elements and highly concentrated industries exist, firms exert control over the price of their product. When these firms are confronted with the costs of environmental improvement, will they absorb the costs out of profits or will they pass the costs on to their customers in the form of higher prices?

The traditional price determination diagram for imperfect competition is used in Figure 4-4 to illustrate the effects when monopolistic elements exist. Before the imposition of the environmental costs (assuming that all costs are variable as in Figure 4-3) the firm is at an equilibrium position in which Price $= P_1$, Output $= Q_1$, and Monopoly Profits $= P_1BCC_1$. After the shift of the curves resulting from the new costs the equilibrium is Price $= P_2$, Output $= Q_2$, and Monopoly Profit $= P_2ADC_2$. Price has increased from P_1 to P_2 as a result of the cost increase, but the price increase P_1P_2 is less than the cost increase DE. Thus, the firm has been forced to absorb some of the cost increase out of profits. Comparing the profit areas indicates that

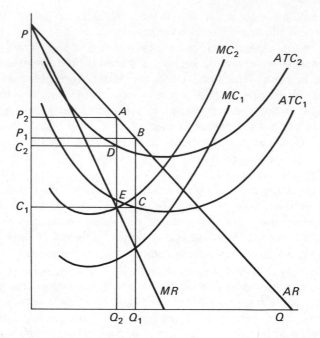

Figure 4-4

the after-cost profit rectangle P_2ADC_2 is less than the pre-cost profit rectangle P_1BCC_1. The monopolist was able to pass on only a portion of his cost increase.

Since perfect mobility is assumed, the effect of the decline in output and employment in the monopoly firm would not create unemployment of labor or capital. Factors no longer employed in this industry would be employed elsewhere.

The portion of the cost increase which can be passed on by the firm depends (all other things being equal) on the elasticity of demand for the product. The effect of the elasticity of demand is illustrated in Figure 4-5. Demand curve D_2 is more inelastic throughout its entire length than demand curve D_1. The pre-environmental cost equilibrium price is P_E and, assuming D_1, the post cost price is P_1. Assuming D_2 is the demand curve, the post environmental cost price is P_1. Thus, the more inelastic the demand, the greater the share of the cost increase which can be passed on to the consumer in the form of a higher price.

The analysis of cases between the perfect competition case and the monopoly case are more complex because the pricing mechanisms of oligopoly and monopolistic competition are not fully under-

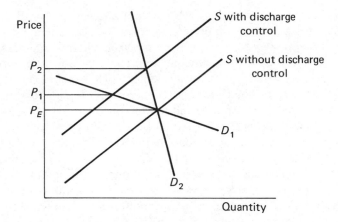

Figure 4-5

stood. If the even more complicated assumption is made that the firm does not operate to maximize profits but has some other goal, a whole new analysis is required.

Immobility Analysis of the problem becomes more difficult when the assumptions of full employment and resource mobility are removed. Environmental improvement will mean lower output and fewer jobs in particular firms, industries, and geographical areas.

Given a lack of alternative employment opportunities, worker investments in specific job-related skills, geographic lack of labor mobility, and the difficulty of learning of employment opportunities in other areas, firms may be able to pass some of the costs of environmental improvement back on to their employees in the form of lower wages. Capital also is frequently immobile between areas and industries, and in many cases the return on capital will be depressed below the normal profit level. These considerations will strengthen the opposition of both labor and capital to environmental improvement.

Incidence and General Equilibrium

The previous discussion of incidence utilized partial equilibrium analyses. In order to assess accurately the incidence of environmental improvement, it is necessary to consider the adjustments in the economy as a whole.

One technique for such analysis, Interindustry Input-Output Analysis, was presented in Chapter 2. The model demonstrated that direct and indirect interindustry output effects could be traced and assessed. Similarly, the use of input-output analysis permits the tracing of the direct and indirect effects on price and cost adjustments.

Only through general equilibrium analysis can the ultimate incidence of the costs of environmental improvement be traced and the ultimate impact of the effort on all sectors of the economy be illustrated. The reader should consider the complexity of the incidence problem in light of the input-output model, because policy making requires that all direct and indirect effects resulting from environmental improvement efforts be known or at least estimated. The detailed, real world analysis of this incidence is beyond the scope of this text. It should be very clear, however, that although the initial impact of the costs of environmental improvement may fall on the polluter, the operations of the price mechanism guarantee that these costs will be shifted by the price mechanism, either fully or partially, to the user of the final product. In addition, those costs not shifted forward to the user of the product will be absorbed by labor and capital. The process of eliminating the environmental problem will not be without its costs to the consumer, the worker, and the capitalist.

Part Two

CONSTRAINTS ON ENVIRONMENTAL

POLICY DESIGN

5

The Compensation Principle and Environmental Policy

The proponents of environmental improvement frequently ignore, or are indifferent to, the fact that their success may be detrimental to other individuals or organizations. They argue that polluters have been profiting from the exploitation of free public environmental resources and that equity requires the polluters to pay for cleaning up their sewage, wastes, and other environmental damage.

Those who stand to lose the most through environmental improvement and preservation insist that the typical program is not fair. They point to lost jobs and fewer dividends; they ask why the costs are very specifically centered on a few individuals while the benefits are widely distributed. The perennial argument associated with environmental legislation centers on the equitable distribution of costs and benefits, including the often nearly immeasurable esthetic, psychological, and ecological costs and benefits.

This chapter examines the equity issues involved in environmental improvement and preservation. Of specific concern is the question of whether or not those incurring losses of income or capital as a result of environmental change should be compensated for their loss. What does society owe to the worker who loses his job when a polluting mill closes rather than meet the more stringent antipollution regulations? Does society have a debt to the mill owner under these circumstances? What is the appropriate distribution of the costs and benefits of environmental improvement? The satisfactory resolution of these issues may be critical in gaining the support of labor and capital for environmental improvement.

The Incidence of Costs and Benefits

Widespread acceptance of a program of environmental change depends upon the political acceptability of the distribution of benefits and costs. The benefits of environmental improvement are widely distributed among the members of the society. Under most proposed programs, however, the costs are heavily concentrated on specific groups — producers of a product, users of a product, or workers in a given industry. Thus, opposition arises from those who feel that they are being forced to bear an "unfair" share of the costs in the form of lost jobs, lost profits, or higher prices.

Suppose I lose my job at the local chemical company in the process of the town's cleaning up the local river. All share the benefits of a clean river, but you have gained access to the clean river at no cost while my access to the clean river has cost me my livelihood. You may regard this as fair because my employment had been depriving you of past enjoyment of the river. I will regard the situation as unfair because, while you swim in the river, I may not be able to find another job and will be trying to support my family on unemployment compensation or welfare.

Fairness is not defined in economic theory. Efficiency is defined with great precision, but the efficient solution is not necessarily fair. Nevertheless, regardless of how efficient a proposed program is going to be, those who feel that they are being "unfairly" treated will withhold their support from the program. The political problem for policy formulation becomes one of lowering the feelings of "unfair" treatment sufficiently to gain the necessary support for the environmental program.

For the purposes of this analysis, environmental issues can be categorized into two broad areas: those situations in which environmental benefits are potential and costs are current (that is, environmental improvement) and those in which environmental benefits are current (and future) and the costs potential (that is, environmental preservation). The distinction is important because of differences in the distribution of costs in the two cases. Additionally, the law seems biased in favor of current, as opposed to potential, uses and rights. From the environmentalists' point of view, this means preservation is different from, and more likely to succeed than, improvement. There are probably good reasons for this apparent bias in the law. Current use is identifiable; potential use is subject to a great deal of uncertainty. Provided that current economic actions are legal, abridgement of a person's, group's or industry's current economic rights is presumed to impose an identifiable loss. On the other hand, abridgement of potential economic rights by placing constraints upon potential economic activity involves an uncertain amount of loss. The opportunity cost doctrine suggests, however, that the loss can never be greater than the difference between the potential gain in the constrained (or outlawed) activity and the gain from the next best alternative. These potential losses are contrasted with the loss of fixed investments (both physical and human) which can result from abridgement of current activities. Because environmental improvement programs often impose current theoretically identifiable costs, it is easiest to begin the analysis with them.

Environmental Improvement Programs and Compensation Problems

Costs of environmental improvement fall into two broad categories: (1) costs of pollution abatement equipment and its operation and maintenance and (2) costs of plant shutdown or product line discontinuance. The incidence and the probability of occurrence of these costs are important for an evaluation of the likely sources of political opposition if the ultimate burden of costs is distributed differently from the final incidence of benefits.

The costs of environmental improvement are not necessarily borne by those legally assigned to bear them. Market and production conditions will determine whether or not the firm will bear the entire cost, whether the firm can pass the costs forward to the consumer or backward to labor and suppliers, or whether some combination of these possibilities will exist. Furthermore, the final incidence of costs depends upon whether or not the incidence of direct costs is borne equally (that is, in proportion to output) by all sellers in the market. If this is not the case, as, for example, when domestic producers are forced to install pollution abatement equipment and foreign competition is not faced with such a cost, the incidence of direct costs will affect the final incidence of costs. (This, of course, is not the only case in which direct costs will be borne unequally by producers.)

The probable final incidence of costs can be illustrated by cross-classification of markets according to the degree of seller price control and the degree of consumer substitution possibilities (in other words, whether the cross elasticities of demand for the industry's product are high or low). When good substitutes for the industry's product are readily available, firms will find that the possibilities for shifting the costs of environmental improvement to consumers are slight. If substitute goods are not readily available, the firm will find that costs can be easily shifted to consumers except in cases in which the direct costs of environmental improvement vary significantly between firms.

An alternative method of examining the incidence of final costs is through a comparison of cost incidence with benefit incidence. To the extent that a firm or industry is capable of shifting the costs of environmental improvement to users of its product, disparities between the burden of costs and receipt of benefits are reduced; but it is unlikely that costs and benefits will be distributed equally to all individuals. For example, if paper mill pollution is abated and the industry passes on the costs of abatement, consumers of paper will pay the costs, but only those people who suffered from the mill's pollution will benefit. Given the position of many environmentalists with respect to the strong interconnections of the environment, the number of people "in contact" with the original pollution may be very large. In that case, if industry can shift the burden of environmental improvement programs to consumers, the incidence of costs and benefits may be reasonably equitable and generate little political reaction.

When industry cannot pass on the costs of environmental improvement, there is apt to be strong and perhaps justified political opposition. The reason for strong opposition should be clear: the costs of environmental improvement are borne only by the industry (owners and perhaps employees) though the benefits are widespread. Furthermore, given American legal codes and the history of enforcement and interpretation of statutes, the opposition is reasonably justified from the point of view of equity. The set of legal regulations is merely one of the many sets of constraints under which a firm must operate. The legal constraints differ from resource, technological, and market demand constraints because the former are the essentially arbitrary result of legislative behavior. The resource, technological, and market demand constraints, which change relatively slowly and are subject to some degree of predictability, allow the firm to respond in such a way as to minimize adverse changes. Legal constraints are capable of instantaneous or at least very rapid change. In many cases, such as the automobile exhaust standards, however, a period of adjustment is established by law. To the extent that the firm's legal constraints change rapidly relative to its ability to respond, firms are more likely to have to bear most of the costs of environmental improvement. In such cases it may be reasonable to argue that the essentially arbitrary action of the legislature is unfair to the affected firms. The legislature has, in effect, changed the rules in the middle (is there an end?) of the game. Clearly, this kind of situation will give rise to strong political opposition to environmental improvement.

A somewhat analogous policy problem, and one whose analysis may help clarify the problem of environmental improvement, arises with respect to tariff reduction. Economists generally hold that free trade is superior (in the sense that it, like environmental improvement, will produce a higher level of economic welfare for the nation) to a situation in which trade is hampered by tariffs and quotas. Given this belief, a reasonable policy is to advocate the elimination of tariffs and quotas. The problem with a free trade policy is that tariff reduction changes the distribution of welfare. Owners and employees in the tariff protected industries are likely to pay most of the costs. As in the case of some environmental improvement programs, this inequitable distribution of costs and benefits can be expected to create strong political opposition to proposed legislative action. Opposition is based on the argument that the legislature is changing the rules in the middle of the game.

Faced with this policy dilemma, economists have generally found recourse in an analysis known as the compensation principle. If a particular policy, such as tariff reduction or pollution abatement, redistributes income, that is, if the incidence of costs and benefits is unequal and if the benefits exceed the costs (as they presumably do in both tariff reduction and pollution abatement), then it should be possible for those who benefit to compensate fully those who bear the costs and still have a net gain. In practical terms, the compensation principle means that tariff reduction or pollution abatement legislation should be accompanied by offers of compensation to persons or industries hurt by such legislation. The Trade Expansion Act of 1962, for example, which anticipated the mutual reduction of tariffs by the major trading nations of the world, employed the compensation principle as a means of reducing the political opposition of workers and firms in industries certain to be hurt by lower tariffs.

The difficulty with such offers of compensation is the real world determination of when a firm or industry bears an inequitable share of the costs. The previous analysis has indicated that losses are most likely to occur when firms are not able to shift the cost burden to consumers. Losses would be expected if environmental improvement legislation imposed unequal costs on producers in the same market or if there were a high degree of consumer substitutability for the industry's or firm's product. Unfortunately, in the real world this neat division of possibilities is not clear. Both the degree of substitutability and the extent to which costs can be shifted vary widely between firms and industries.

Firms in the same market may face different cost changes as a result of environmental improvement. For example, the age and technology of a particular plant often affect the costs of pollution abatement. In the paper industry, effluents from older plants are significantly more difficult to clean up than those from newer plants. Costs of water or air pollution abatement also vary according to the production process. Differences in the direct cost burden are also likely to occur when environmental improvement legislation is regional or national and the industry market is national or international. Differences of these sorts lead to a whole range of differences in the incidence of direct environmental improvement costs, and, necessarily, to great differences in the opposition of various firms to environmental legislation.

From a practical point of view, these wide variations can pose difficult problems of identification. For example, at the same time that the environmental rules affecting the firm are changing, other constraints are also changing. An old paper mill might close down with a very loud denunciation of new pollution abatement legislation. It would be very difficult to determine whether the pollution abatement legislation was in fact the cause of shutdown or merely a management pretext for closing a deteriorating and obsolete plant. Perhaps the pollution abatement legislation merely accelerated an already imminent closing. It would also be very difficult to determine the extent to which a firm was not able to shift the burden of pollution abatement costs to its customers. Measures of the ability and willingness of consumers to change to substitutes for the firm's or industry's product are very difficult to obtain. How, for example, could one reliably segregate a loss of sales because of pollution abatement costs (and thereby higher prices) from other changes in costs (and prices) or, for that matter, from long-term changes in consumer demand, changes in the quality or style of product, changes in sales promotion, and so on? Identification of the industry's or firm's share of the final cost burden of environmental improvement legislation is likely to be nearly impossible in a practical sense. Nevertheless, if the idea of compensation is to have a practical application, it is necessary to find a practical way of deciding whether or not the incidence of the pollution cost burden is responsible for the firm's problems.

The basic intent of the Trade Expansion Act of 1962 seems to be to offer compensation only to those firms forced to shut down because of tariff reduction. Proof of damage consists of plant shutdown. This may seem to be a rather harsh criterion, but there are good reasons for its use. Assume, for example, that a firm is able to shift only a part of the costs of pollution abatement to consumers. There are two possible courses of action open to the firm: it can absorb the remaining costs or it can shut down. The course chosen by the firm would depend upon its profit situation at the time the legislation became effective. If the firm's operations were marginal, if it were just covering its average variable costs, one would expect it to shut down immediately if the added costs raised average variable cost above the firm's marginal revenue. The capital loss to the firm would constitute *prima facie* justification for compensation. If the increase in the firm's costs did not make it impossible to cover average variable costs but reduced profit to a below normal level, one would expect an eventual shutdown. The capital loss in this case would result from the reduction of the expected lifetime of the firm's current equipment. If environmental improvement legislation offered compensation for the value of the capital loss suffered by the firm, a firm in the position just described would be faced with a difficult decision. The compensation for the value of its capital loss (the undepreciated value of its equipment and buildings less resale value) would have to be balanced against the possibility that continued efforts at cost reduction might restore normal profit levels. If the firm chose to continue operating, there would be no *prima facie* evidence that pollution abatement costs were too burdensome; if the firm chose to shut down, the shutdown would constitute *prima facie* evidence that management regarded pollution control costs so burdensome as to remove all hope of achieving future normal profits. Compensation would be warranted in this instance.

In a third possible situation, the firm could find that pollution abatement costs were not large enough to cause profits to fall below the normal level. The pollution abatement costs might be small or shiftable to consumers, or profit levels might be high enough to cover even large unshiftable costs. In the latter instance, pollution abatement costs constitute a lowering of the value of the firm's return on its capital — that is, there is a capital loss of sorts. Is this cause for compensation? The answer is generally no. Economists recognize several instances in which profits can be above normal. In a perfectly competitive market profits can be above normal during a period of expansion. High profit levels in an industry serve to attract new entrants and a future expansion of supply. High profits are, in effect, a reward to entrepreneurs for fulfilling consumer demands — presumably a socially useful function. Given the external diseconomies represented by pollution, however, the price of the industry's product is generally lower than the price which would prevail if all resources were costed inputs. The polluting industry, which is not paying for all of the resources being used, will expand supply beyond the socially desirable level. If pollution abatement legislation accurately prices air and water resources, expansion of the industry will cease, or at least slow down, and profits will fall more speedily to normal. Pollution abatement legislation will, in fact, reduce the expected profits of the firm but only to the extent that it forces the firm to pay for all its resources. A firm which can continue to make at least normal profits after pollution abatement legislation is only denied the windfall profits which would have resulted from environmental exploitation. Compensation would not be warranted in such an instance.

Higher than normal profits can also occur in industries in which entry and supply are in some way restricted. In the cases of oligopolies, monopolies, or monopolistic competition, pollution abatement costs also reduce the expected profits of the firm and as such constitute a capital loss of sorts. Is there a need to compensate firms for the loss of monopoly profits? It would be difficult to find anyone other than the firms themselves to argue such a case. A refusal to give compensation leaves the burden of costs on the firms and does not reduce their political opposition to environmental improvement legislation.

Environmental legislation can also have a strong effect on labor. The impact on labor is, of course, intimately tied to the impact of the legislation on the firms employing the labor. If a firm is forced to shut down, labor is obviously affected; if firms can pass on all the costs of pollution abatement to consumers, labor will be unaffected. The need, or lack of need, for compensation in these two instances is clear. In instances where firms do not shut down and do bear at least part of the burden of pollution abatement costs, however, the effect on labor is ambiguous, because firms may be able to pass these costs backwards to their employees. Higher variable costs may cause firms to reduce output and employment. On the other hand, the need to operate and maintain pollution abatement equipment implies the need for more labor. These opposing effects may be small and self-cancelling and therefore not really worth worrying about when compared with the unemployment created by shutdowns.

The issue of compensation for labor affected adversely by pollution abatement legislation is complex. When a plant shuts down, a worker can lose a great deal. He may lose a certain amount of income until he finds another job; he may lose a certain amount of his own "human capital" (that is, skills and productive knowledge) which is tied specifically to the shutdown firm; he may lose seniority and pension rights; he may be forced to move and to give up his house and friends. How is one to establish a measure of the extent of his loss? Some of the worker's losses, such as income while unemployed, are measurable; but many of his losses are not. The Trade Expansion Act of 1962, a piece of legislation relevant to this question, ignores these immeasurabilities — probably a very wise course of action. Instead, the Act calls for uniform, but rather generous, compensation for displaced workers — 65 percent of the average industry wage for a period up to two years and relocation and retraining allowances. The purpose, of course, is to ease the dislocation costs borne by workers.

Will, then, compensation to labor and capital raise the political feasibility of environmental improvement programs? Will compensation practices work? The answers depend on answers to further questions. Are there bases for compensation which will produce both equity and the feeling of having been treated equitably? If the compensation is offered to marginal firms which shut down, will the owners of such firms view compensation as merely a convenient and lucrative way to "bail out." These firms may even begin to argue *for* environmental improvement legislation. Compensation that is "more than fair" can remove the political opposition to environmental improvement. A similar behavioral phenomenon may be observed in urban renewal programs. Current businesses are given a choice of selling out or rebuilding. Since purchase prices are often set very high, many marginal businessmen jump on urban renewal as a rather prosperous way to go out of business. It beats dreary fire sales any day!

All firms, however, are not marginal. As a general rule, pollution abatement costs represent a small proportion of total costs (see Chapter Three) and the likelihood of shutdowns is small. Some firms will be able to shift all the costs of pollution abatement to consumers, though most will have to absorb some of the costs. Given the shutdown criteria, the possibility of compensation is likely to have little attractiveness to firms with no intention of shutting down. Consequently, the offer of "fair and reasonable" compensation for shutdown, though it may create certain factions within the business community, is not likely to reduce opposition to pollution abatement, because most firms will not be forced to close.

Similar offers of adequate compensation to labor could produce high political dividends. The labor movement in general seems to be torn between a strong desire for a clean and livable environment and the possibility that plant shutdowns will cause economic losses to many workers. Antienvironmental propaganda, leaving the impression that such shutdowns are likely to be widespread, has fostered a great deal of worker ambivalence toward environmental improvement.

Though there will probably not be the massive shutdowns and large need for compensation feared by many, the offer of compensation reduces labor's economic uncertainty and increases labor's support for environmental legislation. In effect, the offer of compensation is likely to remove the rather effective threat of payroll blackmail from the repertory of the antienvironmentalists.

A practical, though not particularly appealing, political solution is to raise the level of, and reduce the criteria for, compensation. It is always possible to turn pollution abatement legislation into, in effect, a huge pork barrel. In fact, this is one of the great dangers inherent in the whole idea of compensation. Anything can be bought. From a technical point of view this practical difficulty with compensation can be traced to the problems inherent in the measurement and determination of the incidence of costs. Given the lack of adequate measurement, there is always a tendency for overcompensation and, probably more important, there is no way to audit the validity of compensation payments.

Environmental Preservation Programs and Compensation Problems

As with environmental improvement programs, environmental preservation is likely to create an unequal incidence of costs and benefits. The difference is that successful environmental preservation legislation produces immediate and future benefits and potential costs. Is the compensation principle applicable or practicable in such instances? In order to answer this question, the nature of costs has to be examined more closely.

Preservation implies that an area or natural environment is closed off to economic exploitation. Potential jobs and profits are denied to persons or firms who *might* have benefited from that particular environment's location or resources. For example, opposition to the location of a refinery on the scenic and clean Maine coast has been considered as opposition to the possibility of economic development — more jobs and higher incomes — in the area. The costs of environmental protection are often seen in terms of a denial of the benefits of economic growth. Does this trade-off exist in fact? If it does, can compensation policies be devised?

In the short run, environmental preservation decreases the size of the set of economic opportunities available to some firms and individuals. In the long run, of course, it is possible that environmental preservation may be the only means for maintaining a non-zero set of economic opportunities. The important questions relate to the amount of reduction of the size of the set and the distribution of lost opportunities among individuals and firms.

The argument against preservation usually stresses both the general loss of opportunities and the theory that the greatest cost burden falls on the poor. The thrust of the argument is that past economic growth has had a tremendous beneficial effect on the standard of living and promises to produce the same in the future; so, if we are to eliminate poverty, it is necessary to have economic growth so that there will be more, not fewer, jobs, goods, and services.

There are two especially important assumptions built into this argument: (1) environmental preservation places a significant limitation upon the set of potential economic opportunities and (2) economic growth, and only economic growth, will, through the process known as "trickle-down," eliminate poverty. Both assumptions are subject to serious doubt.

The first assumption can be dealt with rather easily. Essentially it is a variant of the old Keynesian stagnationist argument. This point of view posits the existence of a very limited set of investment opportunities. Continuing investment reduces the quantity and quality of investment opportunities. Economic growth, as a result, becomes increasingly more difficult over time. Eventually, the set of investment opportunities becomes so small that growth is choked off and stagnation results.

When applied to environmental preservation, there is a certain amount of halftruth to this position. If a new industrial plant is required to meet very stringent environmental protection regulations, the added equipment, maintenance, and operating costs will lower the rate of return on the firm's investment and increase the probability that the investment will not be made. The fact that environmental protection regulations will create new investment opportunities in industries producing environmental protection equipment is conveniently ignored. If environmental regulations prohibit clearcutting of forest resources, the rate of return to lumbering and pulpwood operations will probably be lowered. Yet the regulation will simultaneously raise the rate of return to investment in alternative, and presumably better, production methods and in substitute product lines. Environmental protection changes the character or allocation of investment but does not necessarily limit the size and quality of the set of investment opportunities.

The second assumption of the argument against environmental protection states that environmental protection is highly discriminatory against the poor, because it is the poor who benefit from economic growth. On an aggregate national level, this assumption is disproved by the above argument that the character, but not the rate, of growth will change. On a local or regional level, however, there is some substance to this assumption. When the character of investment changes, the location of investment activity may also change. A particular area or region may find that environmental protection means the loss of potential jobs and income.

Will poor people bear the costs of environmental preservation through loss of potential jobs? Is the solution of one social problem likely to give rise to another? The answers depend, to a large extent, upon the relationship between the character of investment and both the quantity and type of jobs created by investment.

The relationship between investment and the quantity of jobs created is usually discussed in terms of factor intensity. Industries are usually characterized by the ratio of capital to labor. Those industries in which relatively large amounts of capital per worker are required are referred to as capital-intensive industries. Industries in which the ratio of capital to labor is relatively low are referred to as labor-intensive industries. These ratios vary greatly from industry to industry, and some industries will provide a larger number of jobs per million dollars of investment than other industries. Given equal sized investments, a capital-intensive industry will provide fewer jobs than a labor-intensive industry. Therefore, the potential cost of environmental protection is greater if labor-intensive industries are discouraged from investing than if capital-intensive firms are discouraged.

In terms of the effects of environmental preservation on the job prospects of the poor, the types, rather than the quantity, of jobs potentially lost is of greater importance. In the offhand manner in which this subject is usually treated, there is often the implicit assumption that a job is a job, and if a new industry locates in a town and employs 200 people that means that there are 200 more jobs. This is more than a bit misleading. First, jobs come in all sorts of different packages. Most require some sort of training, skill, experience, or education. Each firm has different requirements for its labor force and in order to meet those requirements must hire people with appropriate skills, training, experience, and education. To a certain extent firms can and will train people if their labor force requirements cannot be obtained in the labor market. The willingness of firms to offer training, however, is constrained by the probability of success from the point of view of the firm. Will the cost be relatively low? Will the increase in productivity be somewhat higher than the cost? Will the trainee remain with the firm after he has been trained? Can the firm find previously trained workers in other localities?

Thus, the potential loss of jobs and income has to take into account, not the number of employment slots proposed, but the number which are potentially available to the people within that locality prior to the proposed date of the new firm's entry. Will the firm require the kinds of skills, training, experience, and education currently available in the local labor force? If the firm's requirements do not conform with the local community's available labor supply, what is the probability that it will import part of its work force? Answers to these questions not only are difficult but will, of course, vary with each particular locality and proposed industry. These losses are costs *only if* local investment is actually curtailed as a result of environmental preservation legislation.

The social magnitude of such costs, especially with respect to its incidence on the poor, is difficult to estimate. Experience with regional economic development programs, however, suggests that the real costs to the poor may be surprisingly low. Regional development programs have not been very successful in generating jobs for poor people. For example, the Appalachian regional development effort with an authorized budget of $1.1 billion had created only 4,500 jobs by 1967.[1] How many of these jobs actually went to poor people rather than in-migrants or the already employed nonpoor is not clear. There seems to be a general impression that deliberate attempts to create jobs for poor people have not been very successful. This experience strongly suggests that the potential loss of jobs for poor people as a result of environmental preservation is likely to be relatively low. Job creation through investment does not seem to be a sufficient condition for the creation of jobs for poor people.

Is compensation appropriate in cases of environmental preservation? Costs of preservation exist. Losses to capital can never be such that the capitalist does not have the opportunity of employing his capital elsewhere at least at the going rate of return. (The distinction between environmental improvement and environmental preservation relegates all instances of capital loss to the former.) The primary costs appear in the form of lost potential jobs in particular localities. It is very difficult, and perhaps impossible, to determine who will lose these potential jobs. There may be some reason to believe that the magnitude of loss is likely to be small, but there will be losses nevertheless.

The idea that losses will be incurred as a result of a public policy suggests that the principle of compensation is applicable. Yet the immense practical difficulty of identifying the exact incidence of the costbearing suggests that compensation may be an unworkable concept. Perhaps the reason for this apparent unworkability of the compensation principle is that the manner and techniques of compensation considered so far implicitly relate to compensation for loss of previously acquired human and physical capital.

Compensation with respect to environmental preservation implies a need to compensate for costs which are only potential (that is, the loss of reduction of economic opportunities). The appropriate compensation may be the provision of potential future alternative opportunities. This alternative idea of compensation may not be any more workable, because the problem of identifying those who deserve the compensation remains. For example, if the provision of training and education for labor is an appropriate practical provision of alternative future economic opportunities, to whom should society offer the training? This would be a very difficult question to answer if the appropriations for training were limited to an amount equal to the expected value of lost economic opportunities.

On the other hand, the purpose of examining the compensation principle is to find ways in which it might contribute to an increased political feasibility for environmental proposals. In this light, the problem of identifying those persons who are likely to pay the potential costs of environmental improvement is not so great. It is important to recognize the existence of these costs and to take steps to minimize their impact in order to reduce the strength of political opposition to environmental preservation. In practical terms, environmental preservation legislation should be accompanied by legislation aimed at raising the potential economic opportunities of all workers in affected regions. Manpower Development and Training Act (MDTA) programs, though with broader coverage and more financing, are the kind of model which might be useful in this context.

This is not a suggestion for a workers' pork barrel. The earlier objections to the pork barrel possibilities of compensation centered on payments to non-shutdown firms earning greater than normal profits. Compensation in such cases merely amounts to a transfer of income to the owners of these firms. No increase in productivity need be associated with the transfer. Provision for greater potential economic opportunities for workers through education, training, and relocation creates the possibility of an actual transfer of income only to the extent that the workers' further education, training, or relocation increases productivity. Only higher worker productivity leads to higher income and an actual transfer of income.

The search for objective criteria of equity has thus far been, and will probably always be, fruitless. The idea of using compensation as a way to grease the political wheels for environmental legislation, or any other legislation, has obvious practical appeal. It also has many practical limitations. Compensation will reduce worker fears and resistance, some cases of employer resistance, and some of the real costs of environmental improvement. Offers of, and actual, compensation may be a fair and reasonable price to pay for labor's support of environmental legislation.

On the other hand, offers of compensation are not likely to be politically effective with respect to capital, except in the few cases of marginal plants. Firms earning above normal profits who have to absorb the costs of pollution abatement are not likely to view a suggested "fair" criterion of shutdown as very fair at all. Their political opposition is likely to continue unabated. One of the dangers of compensation is that once the idea of buying off political opposition with the public purse becomes implanted in people's minds, it is difficult to limit actual payments. The results could lead to magnificent pork barrels which would redistribute income to the owners of capital. From a pessimistic point of view, suggesting the inclusion of the compensation principle in environmental legislation may be like suggesting that a new Pandora's box be opened.

6

Macroeconomic Constraints on Microeconomic Environmental Policy

The development of a specific program for environmental improvement is a microeconomic problem. The microeconomic program, however, must be conducted within a framework which permits the simultaneous achievement of society's general macroeconomic objectives. Resistance to the costs of environmental change is increased by fears that environmental improvement will lower employment levels, raise prices, reduce the rate of economic growth, and lead to a balance of payments deficit. Designing and implementing an effective environmental improvement policy requires not only that these problems be considered theoretically and estimated quantitatively, but that they be adjusted for in policy design.

This chapter examines the possible macroeconomic constraints on microenvironmental policy. The analysis considers questions on a theoretical basis but also draws on the limited supply of empirical evidence bearing on the macroeconomic implications of environmental policy. Does a condition of less than full employment impede progress towards environmental goals? How will environmental improvement affect the components of aggregate demand — consumption, investment, government expenditures, and net exports? Will investment financing problems restrict pollution control expenditures? Will environmental improvement increase inflationary pressures? Will the aggregate effects of an environmental improvement program require macroeconomic policy changes to maintain full employment?

Full Employment and Environmental Improvement

A failure to achieve full employment will constitute a very strong constraint on a program of environmental improvement. Full employment is desired for many economic and noneconomic reasons and it is difficult to believe that the general public will accept substantially less than full employment as one of the costs of environmental improvement. Full employment is a critical — if not a sufficient — condition for environmental improvement.

Full employment facilitates the reallocation of resources which will be required by an environmental improvement program. All studies of the effects of environmental controls have indicated that some plants will be shut down as a result of environmental protection regulations. Probably the most important requirement for lessening the resistance to the controls which will result in plant shutdowns is the maintenance of full employment. The resistance to change of labor and capital can be reduced most easily if the aggregate demand for labor and goods is sufficient to absorb idled workers and create new, productive investment opportunities.

Prosperity eases the problems of internally financing corporate environmental projects. Internal sources of funds, especially retained earnings, will be more plentiful if profits are high and rising than if business is poor and profits are declining. A thriving business sector should lower industry resistance to strict and expensive environmental controls.

External financing of the costs of pollution control will also be easier during a period of prosperity. Expenditures to be financed by new issues of stock are made more willingly during periods of high stock prices and high price-earnings ratios. While interest rates on debt issues are frequently high during periods of prosperity, the improved credit worthiness of the firm may provide a partially offsetting influence on interest rates.

The operating costs associated with antipollution investments can be absorbed into the firm's cost structure more easily during a period of rising earnings than during a period of depressed earnings and strict cost control measures. While the firm may be reluctant to incur new continuing costs during a recession — while earnings are declining and shareholders are unhappy with management performance — prosperity increases the probability that rising profits can be achieved even with increased operating costs.

Research and development efforts within the firm and in the business community as a whole are more likely to be undertaken and well financed in a period of high employment. Much basic and applied research must be done in coming years to develop new and less expensive ways to produce goods without producing pollution and to discover ways of reducing the impact of existing pollution sources.

Consumer resistance to the higher prices which will result from the costs of pollution control should be less during periods of rising real incomes and full employment than during periods of stable, or falling, real incomes and extensive unemployment.

Finally, government expenditures for pollution control and the administration of environmental programs will be higher during periods of high employment. The tax revenues of most governmental units are sensitive to changes in the level of national income. While Federal government deficits are expected and accepted during business recessions, there is some reluctance to expand programs during a recession unless the program is politically popular or is concerned with creating more jobs. Thus, a period of full employment and rising government revenues is more favorable to the expansion of government financing of environmental programs. On the state and local government level, depressed business conditions tend to influence voters to reject bond issues to finance new capital expenditures.

While the case for full employment is strong, there are some points for the argument that less than full employment will lead to a cleaner environment. Interest rates, for example, are usually lower during periods of business recession, and corporate bond financing is therefore less expensive. The positive effect of cheap, readily available credit, however, may be offset by corporate reluctance to incur new debts during a period of economic decline and uncertainty.

Furthermore, full employment may cause more than proportionate increases in pollution levels. As the economy moves closer to full employment, many industries have to reactivate older, less efficient, plants which create more pollution. The steel industry uses older facilities only during periods of high steel demand. These plants are apt to cause more pollution than plants constructed or modernized since the growth of environmental concern.

Also, the pressures to expand to meet rising demand during periods of prosperity may result in greater reluctance on the part of businesses to divert funds needed for expansion to projects designed to improve the environment. Facing a backlog of orders for its products, the firm may resist diverting funds and personnel to environmental projects.

Finally, the capital equipment needed for projects to reduce pollution will rise in price more rapidly when the capital goods industries are swamped with orders. In addition, the lag between capital goods orders and delivery will increase in periods of prosperity.

While the "disadvantages" of full employment are logical, the pressures for full employment are greater. Even if the "disadvantages" of full employment were greater than the environmental advantages, society would probably opt for full employment. Therefore, the impetus full employment will give to efforts to improve the environment will serve as one more imperative for improved macroeconomic performance in coming years. While the maintenance of full employment is no guarantee of environmental improvement, the case seems clear that the path to a cleaner environment will be much smoother under conditions of full employment.

Aggregate Demand and Environmental Improvement

In the basic Keynesian model of income determination used in most introductory textbooks, the level of income and output is determined by the level of aggregate demand. Aggregate demand is composed of consumption, investment, government spending, and net foreign demand. As the components of aggregate demand change, the level of national income changes. Thus, an assessment of the macroeconomic impact of environmental improvement must contain an analysis of the effects of environmental policy on these critical macroeconomic variables.

Two basic points, however, should be kept in mind. First, resource reallocations will permit increases in environmental expenditures without any change in the level of aggregate demand. For example, a reduction in government spending by $10 billion which is offset by added business investment of $10 billion would, except for possible transitional problems, have no net effect on aggregate demand. Second, increases in aggregate demand can be accommodated without creating inflationary pressures if the economy is not already at a full employment level of income and output. Alternatively, if the economy is already at full employment, increases in aggregate demand create inflationary pressures whether the increase in demand is for environmental protection or any other purpose. The level of aggregate demand must be properly managed to accommodate changes in the components while avoiding both unemployment and inflation.

Consumption and Pollution

The macroeconomic study of consumption must begin with a consideration of the measurement of income and consumption. The methodology of constructing this sort of economic data leaves much to be desired. The government's national income accounting data include as consumption the individual's purchase of goods and services from business firms plus imputed data for some transactions which do not pass through the marketplace.

The major failure in the measurement of consumption is the inclusion of purchases of goods and services without regard for any other factors which influence the welfare of the consumer. If fresh air is purchased at a vending machine, as it can be in Japan, it counts in GNP, but if we have an abundant supply of "free" clean air, our use of that air does not count as consumption. If we are forced to breathe foul air, our consumption of goods and services as measured by the government does not change (unless we react by purchasing a gas mask), but certainly our welfare as consumers is reduced. Thus, we need a new measure of consumption which subtracts all "goods" which lower our welfare and adds all goods which are not sold but yet increase our well-being. This "net" measure, while presenting great measurement problems, would certainly be a more comprehensive assessment of consumer welfare than the limited monetary measurement of consumption currently used.

The process of improving the environment will cause an increase in the prices of goods if environmental improvement is financed by the private sector or will cause a decrease in after-tax income if environmental improvement is financed by the public sector. Using the monetary measurement of consumption, the consumer will have reduced purchasing power because of environmental protection. Either he will have less money income available for spending or he will find that the prices of goods have increased. Unless he is willing to reduce his level of saving, his consumption of goods and services will decrease. If we use the "net" measure of consumption and assume environmental improvement, however, the consumer will be consuming fewer, or higher priced, goods having positive utility but will not be forced to consume goods having negative utility. The consumer's welfare may be increased even though he has fewer goods.

The effect of environmental improvement on the level of aggregate consumption depends on the reaction of consumers to changes in the form of their consumption and income. If consumers desire a fixed level of goods and services regardless of environmental quality, then an improvement in environmental quality will cause an increase in the money value of measured consumption owing to price rises or will cause a decrease in the level of savings out of after-tax incomes owing to tax increases. Alternatively, the consumer may regard environment as one of his consumption goods and will maintain a constant level of consumption, the consumption of goods and services decreasing as the level of environmental consumption increases.

If environmental improvement affects prices and if consumers desire a fixed quantity of goods and services, the total demand for measured goods and services remains the same in real terms, but money consumption demand increases. If the cost of environmental improvement is paid by higher taxes, the level of consumer demand remains the same in both money and real terms and the level of savings decreases.

Alternatively, if consumers accept a cleaner environment in place of goods and services, the real demand for measured goods and services will decline. The decline in real demand will be composed of either a decrease in money demand — if environmental improvement is financed by the government — or an increase in prices with money demand constant — if environmental costs are included in the price of goods.

A final consumption problem is related to the operation of the multiplier. Assume that the economy is operating significantly below the full employment level. As part of its attempts to restore full employment, the government increases the level of environmental spending. National income increases by an amount equal to the increase in government spending times the multiplier. The resulting increase in consumer incomes will be partially spent and partially saved. The problem concerns the nature of the goods which are purchased with the increased income. If goods having a high level of income elasticity of demand are also high pollution producing goods, the attempt to improve the environment will result in new damage. For example, the demand for automobiles is considered to be highly income-elastic and automobiles are also great contributors to air pollution. Naturally, the net gain for the environment will be greater if the increase in government spending is for environmental improvement rather than for some other purpose. Unfortunately, even the creation of income in the process of environmental improvement will increase the demand for some polluting goods and partially offset the gains from the anti-pollution spending.

The effects of environmental improvement on consumption, then, will depend on the consumer's reaction to changes in the prices of goods and his after-tax income, his desire to maintain constant living standards in terms of measured goods and services, and the income elasticity of demand for pollution producing goods.

Capital Investment and Environmental Improvement

Probably the most critical determinant of the rate of progress in improving the environment is the level of private capital investment in pollution prevention. An estimate of the total amount of investment required is difficult to make because of the many assumptions upon which an estimate must be based. The Council on Environmental Quality estimates a total of $26 billion (1971 dollars) between 1972 and 1976 will be required to bring existing plants up to existing air and water quality standards and to create new facilities.[1] This represents an annual average outlay of $5.2 billion compared to $170 billion per year in gross private domestic investment and to $120 billion per year non-residential investment (plant and equipment expenditures). Thus, on a very macro level, the level of outlays does not appear to be high. As was indicated in Chapter 3, however, the costs of environmental improvement are not equally distributed between industries.

How will firms react to these new demands on their limited investment funds? The major points in the consideration of this question can be examined by reference to two basic investment theories: the accelerator mechanism and the marginal efficiency of capital analysis.

According to the accelerator mechanism, the level of investment is a function of changes in the level of demand for final output. If the level of investment is a simple function of this sort, a rapid growth of demand for final output would produce a high level of investment. Assuming that the increased demand would result in the building of new productive facilities designed to have less adverse impact on the environment than older plants, a rising fraction of output would be produced under nonpolluting conditions. In the opposite case, lack of increase in the demand for final output would mean less new investment and continued production using older, pollution producing plant and equipment.

The simple accelerator mechanism cannot, however, account for all new plant and equipment investment. Many investment projects are undertaken as a result of cost-reducing technological changes, the obsolescence of existing equipment, and the need for facilities to produce new products. This autonomous investment is not related to the level of, or changes in, total demand. The level of autonomous investment will be affected by stricter regulations against environmental pollution, because stricter regulations will make a portion of existing capital equipment obsolete.

Capital equipment may be discarded before it is physically worn out. As capital goods age they become of relatively less use to the firm for a number of reasons. A firm may sell or scrap machinery because of high maintenance costs. The machinery may become mechanically unreliable and produce a defective product or frequently break down, in either case disrupting the production process. Finally,

technological changes may result in the introduction of a more efficient method of producing the product. Thus, the economic life of
capital equipment is usually less than the physical life of capital, and
the obsolete capital is either sold or held in reserve for use in periods of heavy product demand.

The emphasis on avoiding pollution also increases the rate of capital obsolescence. Many firms, comparing the cost of constructing
new facilities designed to avoid pollution with the cost of modifying
existing equipment to reduce pollution, will find that the lowest cost
method calls for the scrapping of existing plant and equipment.

The steel industry is an example of the capital obsolescence effect
of tougher pollution laws. Open hearth furnaces were once the major
producers of steel, but are gradually being replaced by basic oxygen
furnaces. Antipollution laws are one of the forces increasing the rate
of change of the technology of the steel industry. A source quoted in
The Wall Street Journal of December 1, 1970,[2] indicated that eight
percent of the open hearth capacity would be closed down before
1976 because of the new emphasis on cleaner air. In the case of the
steel industry, the change in technology is being forced by growing
competition from foreign producers but is being accelerated by environmental concern. In other cases, such as in the automobile industry, an unanticipated change in technology may be required.

The modified accelerator theory that incorporates both autonomous
and output-induced types of investment suggests that some antipollution investment will take place regardless of the level of economic
activity and that additional new nonpolluting plant and equipment will
be produced in response to a growing level of demand for final output.

The simple accelerator mechanism fails to take into account two
other economic realities. First, there is a ceiling to the short-run level
of output in the capital goods industry. Even if there were a great
rise in demand for final output, only a limited quantity of new plant
and equipment or pollution control equipment could be produced in
a given period of time. For the environmental improvement effort,
the limitations of the capital-goods industries mean that the transition
to nonpolluting production cannot be achieved over night.

Second, the simple accelerator mechanism does not take into account any of the financial variables involved in the firm's decision-
making process. There is no allowance for the fact that some investment projects may be more profitable than others and thus will have
a higher priority claim on the firm's financial resources. In addition,
the accelerator mechanism does not allow for changes in the firm's
cost of funds.

The more traditional line of investment analysis involves a comparison of the profit and cost of each possible investment project. The profit maximizing firm is expected to invest in all projects which promise a rate of return greater than the cost of the funds needed to make the investment.

Stricter pollution control will have two effects on investment. First, pollution control will change the firm's evaluation of future investment projects. Second, pollution control will require that additional investment funds be used to bring existing plant and equipment up to the newly imposed antipollution standards. Each of the two effects changes the level of investment in different ways.

With respect to the evaluation of future investment projects, the higher environmental standards will increase the cost of each possible investment project which involves a potential pollution problem. While the cost of each project will increase, the operating costs associated with the operation and maintenance of the pollution control equipment will lower the dollar returns expected from the project. Both of these factors will lower the rate of return on projects presenting environmental hazards. When the firm ranks all of its possible investment alternatives, those projects involving antipollution costs will rank lower than they would have had the antipollution costs not been included in the analysis. Thus, all other things being equal, the firm should be led to invest in fewer projects presenting pollution hazards.

The second effect of pollution control deals with existing plant and equipment. Many firms, already having invested large sums, will have to spend additional funds to bring their plants up to the new standards. In this case, the computational system is more abstract than the one used in the previous example. If the firm invests additional funds in pollution control at existing plants, there will be no additional sales revenue to the firm. What return is there to enter into the rate of return equation? There are a number of possible monetary and nonmonetary gains which can be predicted on a theoretical basis. For example, the nonmonetary gains in community or consumer goodwill may be valuable to the firm. Alternatively, not making the investment in antipollution equipment may subject the firm to fines or effluent charges, and the return from antipollution investments would be the avoidance of the fines or charges. In another case, failure to make the investment may result in the plant being closed down by the government and the loss of all profits. Therefore, while there are no direct profits from making environmental investments in existing plant and equipment, there are gains which have a monetary value to the firm.

The firm planning its investment strategy must calculate the rate of return resulting from bringing existing plants up to environmental standards. These investment projects will be ranked in order of rate of return along with the proposed new investment projects. The cost of investment funds will be determined; those projects having a rate of return less than the cost of funds will not be undertaken. In considering the upgrading of existing plants, the firm will find that in some cases it will be cheaper to pay pollution fines or to close down the plant than to undertake the necessary new investment.

The rate of return analysis assumes that investment is responsive to changes in the cost of funds. If the cost of funds — often called the interest rate although the two terms are not completely interchangeable — increases, projects which formerly yielded a rate of return greater than the old interest rate may suddenly yield a return less than the present cost of funds.

The extent to which changes in the cost of funds will affect the process of environmental investment cannot be determined at this time. If the interest elasticity of pollution abatement projects is high, periods of high interest rates will inhibit efforts to improve the environment and periods of low interest rates will encourage these investments. If the interest elasticity of this type of investment is low, changes in the interest rate will not affect the pace of environmental improvement.

A final investment consideration involves the extent to which the necessity of making investments in pollution control will displace other types of investment. If firms are forced to make extensive investments in pollution control, there are a number of ways in which this could affect other types of investment. First, the cost of capital goods may be increased by the added demand for capital goods to combat pollution. Thus, the expected rate of return on other investment projects would be reduced. Second, the demand for funds for investment in antipollution projects may increase the cost of funds and eliminate from consideration those projects previously having only very marginal acceptability.

Simulations using the Chase Econometric Model which were performed for the Council on Environmental Quality indicate that the above factors will indeed have an effect on total investment.[3] Adding the $26 billion of environmental investment to a baseline level of investment indicates that total investment over the period 1972–1976 will increase by only $9.6 billion. This finding indicates that environmental investment will displace a considerable portion of the investment which otherwise would have taken place. In the period 1976–1980, the model indicates that total investment would be less than the baseline projection. Apparently, the termination of the environmental investment will not be fully offset by a recovery of other types of investment. Within this econometric simulation of the effect of the added investment, an expansionary government policy is required to bring the system up to the baseline projection. Thus, the effect of the environmental investment tends to be less stimulative than would be expected. The interest rate effect is also apparent in the Chase simulations. The level of housing starts would decline below the baseline level for the period 1972–1976. The findings indicate that environmental protection is not neutral in a macroeconomic sense and that the achievement of environmental goals is going to present problems for other aspects of economic policy.

Government Spending and Environmental Improvement

The potential cost of environmental spending by all levels of government is both huge and indeterminate. The considerations determining the actual amount of spending include a host of related economic and social factors.

The magnitude of governmental expenditures on pollution control depends on the ultimate decisions relative to the appropriate division of costs between the private and the public sectors of the economy. Some costs, such as solid waste treatment and disposal, are clearly governmental costs; however, the responsibility for the costs of cleaning rivers, for example, is not so clear. Some would argue that because private industry has been responsible for much of the pollution, it should bear the cost. Industry would argue that it does not have the financial ability to undertake comprehensive programs and that some level of government must bear much of the burden. The ultimate division of responsibilities between the various levels of government and the private sector of the economy will be a critical determinant of the level of government expenditures on environmental improvement.

The financing capabilities of the various levels of government differ. If the entire public responsibility is to be assumed by state and local governments, substantial improvements in the quality of air and water will come about slowly. The tax base of state and local governments is already overburdened with the costs of education and welfare, and these units of government are unlikely to be able to absorb any great share of the total cost of environmental improvement unless a revenue sharing or grant program transfers some costs to the Federal government.

Furthermore, the Federal government will have to decide to reallocate expenditures towards improvement of the environment. While the critics of various government programs — especially military programs — argue that funds could be diverted from these programs to environmental improvement, there are many competing uses for any funds which are released from old programs. While the environmental concerns are certainly critical, there are other programs — poverty, health care, and education, to name only a few — which also need additional funding.

Another unknown is the extent to which taxpayers will accept higher taxes to finance environmental improvement. Everyone argues that the government should do more to correct past environmental abuse. Taxpayers, however, may be unwilling to reduce their consumption and savings to finance the necessary new programs. If the rate of taxation is not increased, the normal increase in tax revenues resulting from economic growth could be sufficient to fund new programs. Growth, however, results in increased pollution and the growth may not be worth the added damage to the environment. On the other hand, if government antipollution programs are not funded by either a reallocation of resources or by increased taxes, then the funds must come from the growing tax revenues produced by a growing economy. The damage done by the increase in output, it is to be hoped, will not be greater than the environmental improvements which can be made with the added tax revenues.

Finally, without tax changes, growth, or spending reallocations, expanded Federal government expenditures will depend on deficit spending. The ability to engage in deficit spending is a function of the current level of economic activity relative to the potential level of economic activity. If the economy is operating at substantially less than full employment, it is possible to increase spending on environmental programs without creating inflationary pressures. For reasons indicated in the first section of this chapter, however, less than full employment is probably detrimental to environmental improvement.

Foreign Demand and Environmental Improvement

The difference between exports and imports is historically the smallest part of aggregate demand, yet this part of aggregate demand is very likely to be affected by environmental improvement because of the effect of environmental protection costs on the prices of goods. An increase in American prices as a result of environmental protection costs which is not matched by similar cost increases for foreign producers of competing goods means that markets will be lost to American goods. Likewise, one of the ways in which American consumers can avoid some of the cost of environmental protection is by increasing their purchases of goods from nations less concerned about the protection of their environment. Thus, environmental improvement poses a threat to the balance of trade position of the United States and any other nation which actively attempts to improve its environment while other nations ignore environmental deterioration for the sake of jobs.

The Chase Econometric Model indicates the possible severity of this international trade aspect of the problem. Without a compensating monetary and fiscal policy added to the model, the trade balance would decline by one billion dollars per year over the period 1972–1976 as a result of the price effects of environmental improvement. Using a corrective policy to maintain full employment leads to greater price increases and a further deterioration of the trade balance to a decline of two billion dollars per year for the period 1972–1980.[4]

The Financing of Antipollution Investment

The method of financing antipollution investments by governments and business firms is a matter of some concern to economists. Most environmental projects are long-term investments and will be financed mainly by long-term sources of funds. Much of the Federal government's contribution will be from current funds in the annual budget, but state and local governments will rely upon long-term bond issues.

The business firm has two sources of funds — internal and external. The internal financing of business investment depends on the cash flow of the corporation. Retained earnings and depreciation allowances are the major sources of internal funds for the corporation. For the corporation planning to finance its investment program out of internal funds, the key variable is probably retained earnings. As the income of the corporation rises — assuming constant dividends and a stable corporate tax rate — retained earnings increase. Alternatively, the decline of corporate earnings in a period of recession — especially when combined with a desire to maintain a constant level of dividends — will reduce the ability of the firm to finance new investment out of retained earnings.

Depreciation retains funds in the business to provide for the eventual replacement of capital equipment. These funds are available to finance new investment. Of key importance is the time period over which equipment can be depreciated. If a machine is written off in eight years instead of ten, during each of the eight years a larger allowance for depreciation is taken, accounting costs are higher, profits are lower, and the tax liability of the firm is reduced. Thus, the liberalization of depreciation regulations increases the retention of funds in the firm and provides a source of investment capital.

To the extent that firms are not able to finance antipollution projects out of internal funds, they will have to rely on the capital markets. For the corporation there are two basic external sources of new capital, equity and debt. In raising funds for pollution control, the bias in favor of bond financing should be very strong. Corporations will prefer bonds because the investment to be made with the proceeds of the security sale will not increase total earnings. If the firm sells additional shares of stock, the per share earnings of the company will decrease. All other things being equal, lower earnings per share will lead to a lower share price.

It can be assumed that the major part of externally financed antipollution investment will be undertaken with borrowed long-term funds. The effect of increased business borrowing on the capital markets and interest rates depends on several factors. The limited statistical evidence indicates that environmental investment, rather than being an addition to other forms of investment, will lead to a significant decrease in other forms of investment as environmental investment increases.[5] The level of business activity will influence total "other" investment demand. In periods of slack business activity, the displacement of other investment probably will be less than the displacement which will occur during periods of high business activity. The level of government demand for funds will also influence the level of interest rates. Government, having an interest-inelastic demand for funds, will cause displacement of "other" investment in periods of high interest rates. Finally, changes in the supply of loanable funds will influence interest rates. There is no a priori reason to believe that the supply of loanable funds will be increased by an environmental improvement program. Theoretically, then, it appears that the net effect of environmental investment on interest rates will be to increase long-term rates and displace some nonenvironmental investment.

The General Price Level and Pollution Control

What effect will greater emphasis on the environment have on the general level of prices in the American economy? The answer to this question depends on both the theory of inflation being assumed and on the general level of aggregate demand.

If a demand-pull model of inflation is assumed, the critical variables are the changes in the components of the level of demand and the pre-existing level of employment. If the economy is operating at, or close to, full employment and the level of demand is increased by investment programs or government spending to improve the environment, inflation will result. If the economy is operating at less than full employment, the addition of environmental expenditures will increase output and employment without increasing prices.

Demand-pull inflation is most likely to occur as a result of environmental improvement under any one of the following conditions:

1. Consumers react to the higher prices of goods by increasing the level of their expenditures so that their material standard of living will stay the same while their "net" standard of living increases as a result of environmental improvement.
2. Business firms add environmental expenditures on top of other forms of planned investments so that the total of investment rises substantially in spite of increasing interest rates. This outcome would be possible under the assumption that investment is interest-inelastic or that the Federal Reserve increases the money supply in order to hold interest rates constant as investment demands increase.
3. Government assumes the burden of financing environmental improvement and government expenditures increase without compensating increases in tax revenues.

Any of these inflationary conditions can be offset fairly easily. Appropriate tax increases will lower consumer demand. Business investment can be reduced by either a tighter money policy or increases in corporate taxes. Government demand can be accompanied by appropriate changes in the level of tax revenues. It seems reasonable to assume, therefore, that excess demand inflation could be treated with the standard monetary and fiscal policy tools.

The cost-push theory of inflation suggests that inflation can occur without the existence of full employment. Stated in terms of the environmental problem, the analysis indicates that increases in costs resulting from increases in environmental protection measures will be passed on to the consumer in the form of higher prices because of the administered pricing situations of many industries. If the cost-push theory of inflation accurately portrays the price-setting mechanism of the economy, inflation can be expected to be a part of the cost of environmental improvement.

Cost-push inflation involves reduction in the level of aggregate demand which will show up in the form of lower levels of employment unless the government ratifies the higher price level by increasing the level of demand. The Chase Econometric analysis seems to accord with the cost-push analysis: the impact of environmental investment is to increase prices and simultaneously to lower the level of aggregate demand and to raise the level of unemployment.[6] In the policy simulations, the government has to increase demand to reduce the unemployment rate and in the process encourages an even more rapid rate of price increase. While the Chase results are only one possible analysis and are influenced by the construction of that particular econometric model, the outcome is certainly well within the realm of possibility.

There is some question as to whether the price increases associated with environmental improvement should be considered as cost-push inflation. They are certainly not cost-push inflation in the normal use of the term as a description of wage-push or profit-push inflation. The price increases arising from environmental improvement are the result of the assignment of costs which have been imposed on society in general to the producers and users of these polluting products. This is not a case of one group attempting to increase its share of national income but rather a case of redistribution of costs.

In light of the unique nature of this upward force on prices, there is some question as to whether anything should be done about the price increases associated with environmental improvement. The increased prices will reduce the demand for products which produce pollution and therefore contribute to a lessening of the problem. In addition, decreases in demand will lower the amount of investment necessary to deal with pollution. Perhaps, therefore, the price rises should be welcomed rather than feared.

The real danger from the rising prices associated with environmental costs is that the effect will be to lower the level of aggregate demand and cause unemployment. Thus, monetary and fiscal policy must be employed to restore full employment at the new, higher price level without creating a demand-pull inflation.

The secondary policy problem is the risk that the price increases resulting from antipollution efforts will be used to justify wage and price increases. As consumer prices increase, labor will demand wage increases to offset the higher cost of living resulting from antipollution costs. Business firms will find that input prices rise and they will use these higher costs as an excuse for seeking higher prices. Wage and price controls may have some ability to prevent this secondary wage-price spiral from developing.

A third theory of inflation is based on the effect of shifts in the composition of aggregate demand. Some environmentalists have encouraged consumers to redistribute their expenditures and avoid the purchase of goods which produce high levels of pollution. Suppose that most consumers followed this advice. If the money not spent on these polluting goods were spent on relatively nonpolluting goods, the demand-shift theory of inflation suggests that price increases would result from this change in the pattern of total demand.

By the standard rules of price theory, reduced demand for the pollution-producing goods should lead to reduced price, reduced profits, and eventual exit from the industry or product line. This sequence of events, however, may not occur. If the firms involved are in administered price industries, they may choose not to decrease their price in the face of declining demand. In fact, their costs per unit of output may actually increase as output decreases because there are fewer units over which to spread the firm's fixed costs. The increased unit costs may be a justification for increasing, rather than decreasing, the price of the product. Therefore, while the output of the polluting products will decrease, there is no certainty that their prices will decline.

If demand for the products producing little or no pollution increases, it would be expected that prices would also increase. While prices are usually inflexible downward, they are certainly flexible upwards; therefore, the prices of the products in higher demand will increase. Standard price theory suggests that excess profits will lead to new entry into the industry, an expansion of output, and a decline in price. However, there are numerous possibilities that may prevent these results from occurring. Expanding industries may have high barriers to entry. If new firms cannot enter the market, output expansion will occur only as the existing firms adjust output to maximize profits. Furthermore, the industries experiencing rapid growth of demand may not be able to expand rapidly in the short run. This situation is particularly relevant to the service industries. For example, regardless of any increase in demand for medical services, the supply of doctors and other health facilities will increase only after a very long time.

Demand-shift inflation could arise as a result of the increase in the price of products which produce pollution. If consumers, recognizing the higher prices, switch away from the products which have high antipollution costs, demand will increase for other products and the price of the other products will increase. The extent to which this problem will arise depends on the price elasticity of demand for the polluting products and the unevenness of the distribution of demand among the nonpolluting products. If all the money not spent on products having environmental costs were spent on one particular nonpolluting product, the price of that product would clearly increase. In the more likely case that reduced demand for the polluting product is reflected in small increases in the demand for all nonpolluting goods and services, however, the price problem should be minor. Price elasticity of demand also depends on the mobility of the factors of production and willingness and ability to expand the supply of the nonpolluting products. If all the demand for nonpolluting goods were concentrated on one product the supply of which was perfectly inelastic, the price of that product would increase. But if the supply of the nonpolluting products can be expanded to accommodate the increased demand at constant prices, there will be no inflation. Finally, demand shifts can be more easily accommodated if they are long run changes rather than sudden shifts in the composition of demand.

Price increases, then, seem to be an expected result of the antipollution effort. Some of the increases are justified by the need to assign the full costs to polluting products. The demand-pull pressures can be avoided by appropriate monetary and fiscal policies and, given that the processes of demand-shift will take place over a long period of time, demand-pull inflation should not be a significant problem.

Full Employment, Environmental Improvement, and Macroeconomic Policy Changes

We have seen that full employment is a desirable precondition of environmental improvement. Will the aggregate effects of an environmental improvement program require macroeconomic policy changes to maintain full employment?

Given that the capital goods spending involved in the environmental improvement effort adds to aggreggate demand whether the spending is done by government or by business firms, the first impression is that a greater environmental effort would increase the level of aggregate demand and lower the level of unemployment. There are, however, negative aggregate effects which may operate to reduce the level of aggregate demand and increase the level of unemployment, thus creating a need for stimulative government spending increases.

First, the level of real aggregate demand will be reduced by the fact that environmental spending will increase the level of prices for many goods. The consumer, spending a constant portion of this income on goods and services, will be able to obtain fewer goods at the higher price levels. Higher prices for capital goods will lower the rate of return on some marginal investment projects and thereby lower the level of private domestic investment. Higher prices for domestic goods will lead to a deterioration of the export competitiveness of domestic industry so that exports will go down and imports will go up. Second, in addition to the price effects, there are possible negative effects through the interest rate mechanism. If the demand for funds for environmental projects leads to an increase in interest rates, those portions of aggregate demand which are sensitive to interest rate changes, such as housing, would be adversely affected. Third, plant closings which will result from stricter environmental controls will obviously lead to higher rates of unemployment.

Under the assumptions of the Chase Econometric Model, the impact between 1972 and 1980 of increased investment and operating costs of the industries studied leads to fairly modest increases in the level of unemployment. Unemployment rises a maximum of less than 0.2 percent above the baseline level. Added spending for environmental improvement changes the levels of investment. Although the level of investment is increased by between $1.8 billion and $3.1 billion each year between 1972 and 1975, after 1975 investment is lower than it would have been had the pollution control investment not been introduced into the model.

Within the context of the Chase model, the effects of antipollution investment reduce the level of net exports by $1.9 billion per year in 1975 and the level of housing starts by a maximum of 90,000 per year. The effect on net exports is a price effect and the effect on housing starts is an interest rate effect.[7]

The policy measures which are selected in the Chase model in order to return the economy to the baseline level of unemployment are relatively large. Government purchases are increased by $3 billion, transfer payments increase by $11 billion, and state and local government payments by $10 billion. Moreover, the policy used for this simulation includes increased government employment and additional reserves for the banking system so that the upward effect on interest rates is reversed. Reflating the economy to return the level of unemployment to the baseline level would have the effect of increasing prices at a more rapid rate and causing a further deterioration in net exports.[8]

The results of the Chase model may or may not be accurate. They do serve as warnings that the process of improving the environment will not be without cost and will create problems for other policies designed to achieve other goals. Environmental improvement is not neutral in a macroeconomic sense.

Macroeconomic Policy Program

The impact of environmental improvement is clearly going to effect all of the components of aggregate demand. The process will require compensating changes in the major policy variables in order to prevent recession or inflation and to deal with the balance of trade problem. Assuming that the predictions of the Chase model are accurate, the government will be faced with problems not dissimilar from the economic conditions of the early 1970s — simultaneous unemployment, inflation, and trade deficits. Dealing with these three policy problems will require a careful policy design. An increase in demand through either fiscal or monetary policy will be needed. Probably the most important element of this general policy is the maintenance of a high level of investment. Policy should be designed to prevent the environmental investment from displacing too large a portion of other investment. This will require avoidance of rising costs of capital goods, maintenance of reasonable long-term interest rates, perhaps additional assistance to the residential housing industry, and other investment incentives.

While general policy must be stimulative, inflation and greater balance of payment deficits must be avoided. To cope with the inflation, some wage and price controls will probably continue to be required. Avoiding a continually rising balance of trade deficit will be more difficult. Obviously the first requirement is inflation prevention. The second is progress toward international environmental agreements so that American exporters will not be forced to bear burdens not shared by their foreign competitors.

A revival of "Operation Twist" might be considered as part of the macroeconomic policy program. This policy, tried during the early 1960s, involves open market operations to lower long-term interest rates and encourage investment while simultaneously raising short-term interest rates to attract foreign capital inflows.

Macroeconomic policy must be designed to permit the achievement of our environmental goals but must not be allowed to create unfavorable conditions for the attainment of other social objectives. The achievement of this delicate balance requires careful consideration of all of the macroeconomic implications of policies to improve the environment.

7

Economic Growth and Environmental Improvement

Those concerned with economic growth and development encounter a number of similarities when they consider the more contemporary problem of environmental improvement. The difficulties of measurement in both areas are monumental and are complicated by the lack of precision in the concepts involved. Both subjects are cross-disciplinary and lack an established body of accepted theory. While poverty and pollution have existed for thousands of years, only recently have they been designated national and world problems apparently capable of solution by the efforts of man. In view of the present rate of progress, however, not everyone is optimistic about man's ability to solve either problem.

Economic growth traditionally has been believed to be the panacea for the world's problems. But economic growth has brought with it pollution of the environment. Are progress and pollution separable or is pollution a necessary cost of economic growth? The analysis to follow considers the relationships between growth and pollution. The reader should not expect definitive or value-neutral answers to the questions the analysis raises. The entire problem is so new and complex that we cannot be certain even that all of the right questions have been asked.

GNP: Gross National Product or Gross National Pollution?

Terms like "gross national pollution" and the "effluent society" are obviously designed to elicit an emotional reaction to the rapidly deteriorating environment in which we all live and die. Nevertheless, there is an element of truth in these terms. It has been estimated that the volume of debris and pollution in the United States doubles about every ten years or by roughly twice the rate of increase in the gross national product. Growth economists have long recognized the limitations of using increases in GNP as an indicator of increased social welfare. Increases in GNP are usually expressed on a per capita basis deflated to net out the influence of price increases. In light of new findings on the volume of pollutants produced each year in the economy, consideration should be given to deflating GNP by some estimate of the value of pollutants produced. Paul Samuelson provides us with a rough estimate of this figure:

Our trillion-dollar GNP may be, in part, an illusion. When we finally pay our way in terms of conservation and in preserving the environment, perhaps we shall have left for ordinary consumption only nine-tenths as much.[1]

Social statisticians, especially those in the more developed nations of the world, should include a negative pollutant value in their calculations because conventional wisdom suggests the existence of a high correlation between the volume of industrial output and the volume of pollutants. In many ways, pollution can be viewed as a negative output jointly produced with normal goods and services in an expanded production function which includes air, water, and space as factors of production along with the traditional ones of land, labor, capital, and technology.

Admittedly, economists are reluctant to break with classical theory. Recently, however, technological change, human capital, and similar unorthodox factors of production have become acceptable to economists because they aid explanation and prediction. For precisely these reasons, an expanded eco-economic production function should include air, water, and space even though they often carry no monetary price tag. Indeed, as has been previously indicated, it is precisely because these nontraditional factors of production have been free, or nearly so, that they have been and are being overused and misused.

The Vicious Circles of Pollution and Progress

Like most social problems, pollution has its roots deep in the past. The United States, for example, has traditionally allocated all resources, including the seemingly unlimited natural resources of the frontier, through the competitive private enterprise system. While this may have served well enough prior to the industrial revolution, these traditions and institutions today are among the root causes of pollution.[2]

Nations traditionally conserve those factors of production which are relatively scarce while they overuse and often abuse those resources which are relatively abundant. In the United States, labor has always been the scarcest resource and land — including water, air, and space — has, until recently, been the most abundant resource. Consequently, the history of the economy is replete with examples of socially inefficient use and depletion of a once seemingly limitless abundance of arable and timbered land, unpolluted air, and fresh water. We mined our national resources on the assumption that the frontier was a bottomless pit of abundance and in the process we reaped a harvest of both wealth and pollution. Throughout the history of the United States, the dominant economic institution, a competitive private enterprise, was accompanied by a public policy of laissez faire. According to one of the earliest economists, Adam Smith, this is the exact combination required to insure economic affluence to man and society:

He generally indeed neither intends to promote the public interest, nor knows how much he is promoting it. . . . [H]e intends only his own security, . . . only his own gain. . . . And he is in this . . . led by an invisible hand to promote an end which was no part of his intention. . . . By pursuing his own interest he frequently promotes that of society more effectually than when he really intends to promote it.[3]

Perhaps ironically, but more likely inevitably, this philosophical justification and advocacy of personal self-interest also led man to promote an end which was not his intention — pollution.

The competitive model in Chapter 4 illustrates the nature of the problem. Each firm is led, by the forces of competition, to lower its private costs of production. The one nonpolluting firm in an industry cannot incur higher costs and still make a profit if its competitors are able to avoid abatement costs by polluting the environment. Thus, unless the process is halted by social action, each firm will attempt to transfer to society as much as possible of its cost of production. A vicious circle of competition and pollution can result. The winner is the firm which pollutes the most (thereby avoiding costs and lowering price), and the loser is the firm which pollutes the least. Of course, society is the ultimate big loser.

This brief history is not intended as a blanket indictment of the "free" enterprise system. It is the competitive process (that is, the mandate to reduce private costs) and the virtual lack of societal control of common property, not private property or progress, which lies at the heart of the problem. It is a known fact that Soviet industry pollutes, United States industry pollutes, in fact, government and consumers everywhere pollute. The poetic justice of this short run, or shortsighted, behavior is that these external costs often return to the polluter in the form of higher factor prices. Too rapid despoliation of water eventually leads to higher water prices, for example. Also, labor productivity is often adversely affected by an unhealthy environment.

Another vicious circle of pollution not considered by classical economists is one best designated as spatial. It is not the absolute amount or type of pollution per se which is important, but the amount and type per area or even per person which is significant. Once pollution begins, it often sets in motion a self-perpetuating spatial circle of pollution. Figure 7-1 shows how pollution originates unequally and distributes itself spatially.

Ecologists tell us that the environment has a self-cleansing ability which breaks down when a certain density level of pollutants is achieved. A high density, as well as a high volume of pollutants, destroys the delicate balance of nature. The environment has a limited carrying capacity, and pollution becomes a problem when these limits are approached — and a disaster when they are exceeded. Nevertheless, once a certain level of despoliation of the environment is reached, a tendency to pollute replaces the conservation incentive. In Figure 7-1, for example, it hardly behooves the residents of Areas 2 and 3 to refrain from polluting the already foul water that flows through their regions — especially if abstention carries a price tag. Consequently, the original nonpolluting Area 2 residents have no incentive to refrain from polluting the already foul air and water and

Figure 7-1

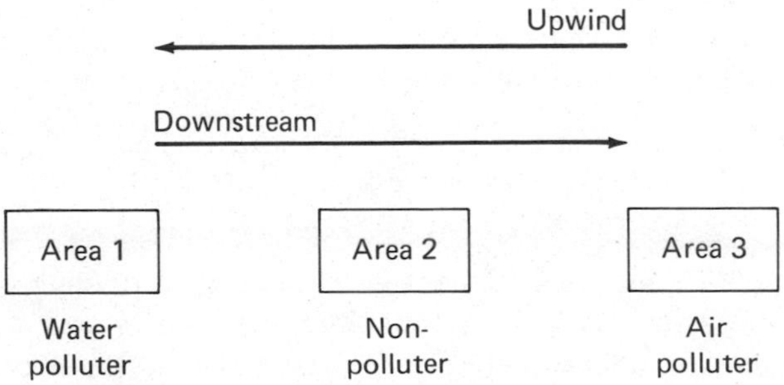

perhaps have an economic incentive to further despoil the environment. Moreover, because the wind shifts and the world is spherical, eventually no one can escape the deteriorating environment. One could interpret the current designation of pollution as a "social problem" as stemming from that time when the wealthy and affluent middle class could no longer spatially escape the deteriorating environment. The poor workers in the mines and mills have always lived with and died from pollution.

One final vicious circle of pollution is associated with technological progress. The modern economy uses different methods of production, produces different products, and uses different raw materials than were used in the past. To be aware of the technological breakthroughs in production, one need only scan a few newspaper headlines under the subject of major pollutants: widespread strip mining, indiscriminant use of pesticides in agriculture, and proliferation of power plants. As consumers, we are all aware of the negative environmental effects of the internal combustion engine, plastics, and elaborately packaged goods of all types. The citizens of the industrialized nations have experienced a seemingly limitless increase in the number of different goods. When combined with new production methods, this increase in quantity and variety of goods contributes to the environmental problem. More underground mining would have resulted in greater pollution, but the introduction of strip mining increased the pollution quotient by some multiple of what it would have been in the absence of this new method of mining. Other examples, such as the internal combustion engine, could be used to illustrate the vicious circle of pollution resulting from new products.

Progress is accompanied by vicious circles of pollution, and while everyone desires the former, no one desires the latter. None of this should be a cause for despair, because the task of breaking these vicious circles of pollution, while difficult, is not impossible.

Is Pollution a Cost of Economic Growth?

One respected authority, Professor E. J. Mishan, in discussing the relationship between growth and the environment has written:

The general conclusion of this volume is that the continued pursuit of economic growth by Western Societies is more likely on balance to reduce rather than increase social welfare.[4]

Needless to say, such a statement is considered economic heresy by many people who have viewed economic growth as a virtual panacea for social ills and have equated increases in real GNP per capita with increases in social welfare. The goal of economic growth has been universally accepted for such a long time that it has become a cult and has left many people blind to the costs associated with growth. This is most unfortunate because competition, efficiency, and growth are not value-neutral or costless social objectives. There are costs and benefits to everything.

Clearly, pollution invariably accompanies economic progress under existing institutions and technological conditions. The real, or opportunity, costs of pollution lie at the crux of the social problem. Opportunity costs constitute the real alternative uses to which the resources expended in production — including air, water, and space — could have been put. If air, water, and land were used only in the production of goods and services for the market, no other costs — money or real — than those of the producers would result from their economic activity. It is virtually impossible to conceive of an economic situation in which alternative resource use opportunities are completely absent.

Economic growth in the United States has given rise to an "overproduction" of produced goods at the expense of the "free" or "public" goods like clean air and water. This misallocation and misuse of resources has reached the point at which many individuals obtain a greater utility from an additional unit of these environmental goods than they do from an additional unit of produced goods and services.

The concepts involved in the relationship between income, the desire for produced goods, and the desire for environmental quality is illustrated in Figure 7-2. The vertical axis in Figure 7-2 measures units of marginal utility and units of marginal disutility. The horizontal axis measures dollars spent on environmental improvement. The downward sloping line labeled MU_{Y_1} measures the marginal utility of dollars spent on environmental improvement when income (Y) is at a level Y_1. The line slopes downward because of the standard assumption that additional units of a given good (in this case environmental improvement) yield smaller and smaller units of additional utility.

The upward sloping line in Figure 7-2, labeled MDU_{Y_1} measures the disutility of spending additional dollars on environmental improvement. The upward slope of the curve reflects the fact that other goods have to be foregone to obtain environmental improvement. The more these other goods must be foregone to obtain environmental improvement, the greater the disutility of giving up additional units of these goods.

The equilibrium point indicates that if Q_1 dollars are spent on environmental improvement, the marginal utility of the environmental ex-

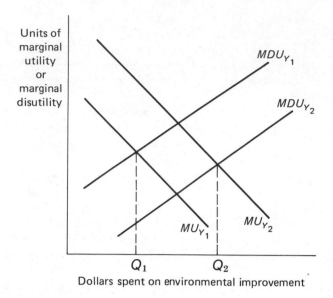

Figure 7-2

penditures will be equal to the marginal disutility of giving up alternative goods. Thus, the society is in an equilibrium position.

Next, consider the effect of a shift in the marginal utility curve from MU_{Y_1} to MU_{Y_2}. It is assumed that the income level Y_2 is greater than the income level Y_1 and that the increase in income leads to a more than proportionate increase in the utility of environmental quality. A given number of dollars spent on environmental improvement provide greater marginal utility when income is Y_2 than when income was Y_1.

Over time the growth of income from Y_1 to Y_2 also shifts the disutility curve from MDU_{Y_1} to MDU_{Y_2}. The growth of income reduces the disutility of spending a given number of dollars on environmental improvement. The new equilibrium at Q_2 equalizes the utility of environmental improvement and the disutility of giving up the consumption of other goods.

Figure 7-2, given the assumptions, indicates that society will be willing to spend more on environmental improvement as income rises. This is a reasonable conclusion. When income is low, the disutility of foregoing the few available goods and services is very high, and, thus there is little interest in environmental quality. As income increases, the marginal utility of additional income (and the goods which can be purchased with the added income) declines, while the marginal utility of the quality of life increases. The analysis, in addition to illustrating that wealthy nations will be more willing to purchase environmental quality than poor nations, illustrates that there is an optimum quantity of environmental quality at any given time and that the appropriate policy does not involve the elimination of all sources of pollution.

Another way of approaching the relationship between growth and pollution involves using a modified Rostow model such as the one depicted in Figure 7-3.[5] The model in Figure 7-3 illustrates a simple and direct relationship between growth and pollution.

In the early, pre-industrial period the peasant engaged in traditional agricultural production was, relatively speaking, a nonpolluter. Most of the inputs, such as seed and fertilizer, as well as the outputs, were naturally biodegradable and were recycled. In addition, the low productivity of traditional agriculture limited the size of the population and insured its spatial dispersion. In contrast, modern industrialized societies consume large quantities of all limited resources, including air and water, and produce an abundance of negative pollution outputs along with the goods and services which have positive utility. In short, the external diseconomies of production, consumption, and agglomeration in the advanced economies of the world are, like everything else, greater in quantity than they were in the past or are currently in the less developed nations of the world. However, because nations and regions have developed at different rates, pollution, like income, is unequally distributed over time, over space, and among individuals and countries. In the underdeveloped nations of the world the rate of increase in pollution may be greater than the

Figure 7-3

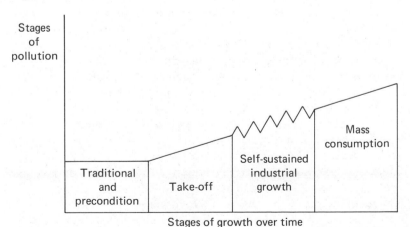

Stages of growth over time

rate of increase in output. Thus, while the income gap between the more and less developed nations may be widening, the pollution gap may be narrowing.

Why, we might ask, are underdeveloped countries polluting at such a rapid rate? To begin with, most decision makers in the less developed nations view economic growth as a panacea to all their problems. Smoking factory chimneys are looked upon as signs of progress and prosperity, but never as polluters. In terms of the analysis in Figure 7-2, individuals in less developed countries realize greater extra utility per dollar spent from an increase in output than from an improvement in the environment. This preference for growth over ecology is such an obsession that it inevitably leads to excesses. Conservation controls are either nonexistent or unenforced in most of these poorer nations, since preservation of the environment is seldom a public policy objective. In short, a public policy of laissez faire exists in the less developed nations with reference to industry and the environment.

This environmental neglect becomes more disasterous because of the industrial structure of the less developed countries. Typically, the modern sector of their economies is characterized by a dominance of primary production. Unfortunately, mining, lumbering, and commercial agriculture are major industrial polluters throughout the world. Moreover, because much of this production is exported, it must compete in the world commodity markets. Consequently, every effort is made to reduce private costs of production in order to be competitive, which invariably leads to the generation of external diseconomies and the creation of a vicious circle of competitive pollution. The nature of their modern industry, competitive world markets, and a public policy of laissez faire combine to create pollution. Does history repeat itself or is man simply slow to learn from his ancestors and neighbors?

Added to all of this is the rapid increase in environmental deterioration in the expanding urban areas of the underdeveloped world. The density of population in cities such as Hong Kong, Calcutta, or São Paulo equals or surpasses that of their counterparts in the industrialized countries. Why should there exist more pollution resulting from size and proximity in these cities than in American cities? One does not have to look far for an answer. The explosive population growth in a relatively short period of time has created demands for public services such as transportation and sewage disposal upon local governments which possessed neither the will nor the funds to deal adequately with the situation. While industry in the United States is migrating from the urban core areas to suburban areas, a reverse migration is occurring in many of the less developed countries. All of this does not portend well for the future of these cities, their countries, or the world's environment.

There are undoubtedly other explanations for the high volume and density of pollution in underdeveloped countries, such as the large, and high rate of increase in population, and the imperfect adaptability of western technology to other economies. There are, of course, factors, such as large agrarian sectors and low levels of output, which mitigate against pollution. Nevertheless, many less developed nations are experiencing the worst of all possible situations — low growth and high pollution. The best policy would be to attempt to increase the volume of produced output while maintaining the quality of the environment.

Are There Limits to Economic Growth?

While the previous analysis indicated that pollution is a cost of growth in the present economic structure of the world, some analyses go further and argue that there are absolute limits to economic growth.

A heated controversy has arisen over the conclusions of *A Report for the Club of Rome's Project on the Predicament of Mankind.*[6] In this report a group of researchers at the Massachusetts Institute of Technology warn that approximately another hundred years of exponential growth at present rates of production, population, and pollution will probably result in a limit to economic growth and then a sudden irreversible decline. Extensive use was made of computers, dynamic systems analyses, and plausible assumptions concerning the relationships between five major variables: population, pollution, natural resources, industrial output per capita, and food per capita. The scientific sophistication of the analysis makes its models and conclusions highly credible.

Contrary to some contemporary opinions, the MIT research team was not composed of alarmists who delighted in extrapolating current world trends of population, growth, and pollution in order to predict man's inevitable self-destruction. Still, many of the results of the various sets of data used in the models were not optimistic. The ultimate limitations of economic growth varied with the assumptions made; the limitations of food supply, exhaustion of natural resources, and growth of pollution all appeared as the villains in various cases. Hoped-for increases in agricultural yield and new discoveries of natural resources postponed only marginally the approach to the limits of growth.

The researchers found that a stable equilibrium state which avoids economic collapse could be achieved only by assuming zero population growth; reducing by three-quarters the current resource consumption per unit of output; the replacement of consumer demands for goods by consumer demands for services; the reduction of pollution by three-quarters; the extension of the life of capital; and the commitment of more resources to food production, the distribution of food, and agricultural conservation. Given these assumptions, per capita levels of food and industrial output are stabilized.[7]

While many objections to the methodology and assumptions of the Club of Rome report have been raised, the work does indicate clearly the threat to world society of the failure to control pollution or to conserve natural resources. The book also indicates the close relationship between the problems of growth and environment:

We affirm that the global issue of development is, however, so closely interlinked with other global issues that an overall strategy must be evolved to attack all major problems, including in particular those of man's relationship with his environment.[8]

Growth as a Solution to Pollution

Given the "limits to growth" problem, can growth continue without, among other things, causing so much pollution as to make the world

Figure 7-4

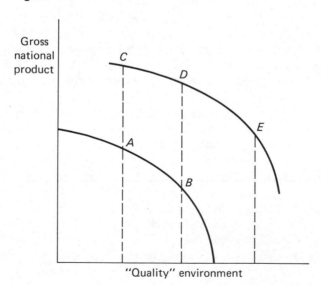

uninhabitable? The pollution problem is being presented today in the mass media as a conflict between industry and ecology, the Sierra Club and the Army Corps of Engineers, and the SST and unemployment. But growth and environmental improvement are not mutually exclusive. The well-known transformation curve illustrated in Figure 7-4 suggests that alternative combinations are possible. For example, economic growth and increased pollution can both be obtained by moving from point B to point C or by moving from point B to point A.

	Alternative	Illustration
1.	Growth and Increased Pollution	$B \rightarrow C$, $B \rightarrow A$
2.	Growth and No Increased Pollution	$A \rightarrow C$, $B \rightarrow D$
3.	Less Growth and Environmental Improvement	$A \rightarrow B$, $A \rightarrow E$
4.	Growth and Environmental Improvement	$A \rightarrow D$, $B \rightarrow E$

By the different allocation of its scarce resources, society may obtain various combinations of national output and environmental quality. Assuming full employment and no increase in resources, a quality environment can be obtained only at the expense of produced goods and services. Fortunately, however, the world is not static and capital increases over time, enabling most societies to have both more produced goods and a quality environment. A new factory with pollution abatement smokestacks producing exhaust free internal combustion engines, for example, would constitute an increase in gross national product and an improvement in the environment. Economic growth per se is not a solution to the environmental problem.

More of the same types of output produced by the same methods is no panacea for either employment, poverty, or pollution. Nevertheless, to improve the environment by reducing the output and consumption of produced goods and services would be unacceptable to most people — especially the poor who are not yet "satiated" with such products to the point where they are willing to consume less for the sake of an improvement in the environment. The life style of Henry David Thoreau at Walden Pond is a realistic alternative for only a very few individuals.

The necessity of arriving at appropriate trade-offs between output and environment is demonstrated by books such as *The Limits to Growth*. The sooner these trade-offs are made and accepted by the world, the better will be the odds of avoiding the cataclysmic collapse of the type described in *The Limits to Growth*. Clearly, the world's resources cannot support the endless expansion of population. The faster population grows, the more resources must be devoted to food production and the faster will be the rate of depletion of nonrenewable natural resources. Thus, the trade-off between population and the quality of life has to be made.

A second trade-off occurs between, on the one hand, the achievement and maintenance of world equilibrium and, on the other hand, vast differences in income distribution. Freezing output at present levels is not a satisfactory solution to the less developed nations. Yet maintaining current growth rates in the developed nations and reaching even higher growth rates in the less developed nations to enable them to catch up will accelerate the process of resource depletion to the detriment of all. Thus, some trade-off seems necessary to increase the standard of living of the less developed nations at the expense of living standards in the more affluent nations.

Yet a third trade-off involves the question of whether the less developed nations should be encouraged to develop along nonpolluting routes. Is their demand for goods so great that they will accept pollution as a cost of growth? It is to be hoped, perhaps vainly, that the developing nations will choose to avoid the problems of the affluent nations and build pollution prevention into their development plans even if the decision lowers the rate of growth of output.

Finally, there must be a trade-off between, on the one hand, current growth and research and, on the other hand, investment designed to find systems and technologies which will enable the world to push further into the future regardless of limits to growth.

While growth and the quality of the environment are not mutually exclusive, future economic growth policies must take more account of the effects of growth on the environment than has been the case in the past. Uncontrolled growth will bring the world to disaster, but lack of growth may condemn billions of people to perpetual poverty. Thus growth must be managed and maintained within the limits dictated by the need for environmental preservation.

Part Three

GOVERNMENT AND CURRENT

ENVIRONMENTAL POLICY

8

Public Goods and Governmental Decision-Making

Chapter 2 indicated that the pollution problem arises from the failure of the market to include in the prices of goods all of the costs of producing those goods. In the case of common property resources, the market is incapable of forcing waste disposers to consider the cost of foregone opportunities — the recreational, esthetic, and life-support uses of the environment which are foreclosed. As a result of this failure, society can now experience a net gain in well-being by devoting some resources to pollution control. At this time society's valuation of the benefits from pollution abatement appear to exceed the costs in terms of other goods that would have to be given up in order to produce pollution abatement. Some measures of the physical magnitude of the pollution problem and of the costs of abating air and water pollution were presented in Chapter 3. Part Two pointed out that abatement policies must be formulated within certain constraints.

This chapter begins the discussion of environmental policy. It is argued that the benefits of pollution abatement are public goods and as such cannot be expected to be provided at optimal levels by a market system. A model of optimal production of public goods is developed and extended to the formulation of antipollution policy. The model will suggest that political decision-making systems must be relied on to select appropriate environmental quality standards. Finally, it will be argued that existing political mechanisms are not particularly well suited to this task and that, as a consequence, the formulation of environmental policy is likely to occur in a disjointed fashion as the body politic discovers, through time, the costs and benefits of past policies.

The response of academic economists, and eventually of the government, to the problem of unemployment provides a model of the steps that must be taken to transform rising concern with environmental problems into effective programs for environmental improvement. Aggregate instability in the market system had been apparent for decades. The rising income trend in advanced capitalist systems was interrupted periodically by recession, depression, and financial panic. The Great Depression of the 1930s was the culmination of successive waves of high unemployment and provided the crisis which so often is necessary for academic and institutional change. In *The General Theory of Employment, Interest, and Money* [1] Keynes demonstrated what the average worker knew all too well: an economy organized in the manner of the developed private enterprise economies of the West would not necessarily produce a full employment level of income. By analyzing the reasons for this failure, Keynes took the first step toward remedying the problem.

Keynes' analysis also specified a set of policy tools which could be used to compensate for the market's failure to assure full employment. Institutionalization of Keynesian policy had to await the development of a data base and a political mechanism which permitted implementation of appropriate policies. The informational basis for policy took the form of the National Income Accounts and the essential machinery for policy implementation was present in the form of Federal taxing, spending, and monetary institutions. The Employment Act of 1946 provided a legal mandate for full employment policies and established the Council of Economic Advisors in the Executive Office of the President as the analysis and policy-design staff. The President's annual *Economic Report* and the Joint Economic Committee's *Hearings,* also required by the Employment Act, serve to focus public and Congressional attention on the Administration's economic stabilization policies and performance.

While analysis, data base, and institutions in the area of economic stabilization are still weak, the academic and governmental response to the problem of unemployment is a model for response to environmental pollution. That is to say, there must be a consensus on the origins of the environmental problem and agreement in principle on the general outlines of its solution. The economic theory of public goods, discussed below, provides the necessary explanatory model, and points out the essential characteristics of optimal environmental policy. Moreover, society must select a set of policies — standards for air and water quality — and design programs for the effective enforcement of those policies. As will be seen in Chapter 11, economics is particularly helpful in program design and enforcement. But the prior question is that of society's capability for making correct decisions about alternative conflicting uses of air and water. This is the question to which we now turn.

The Problem of Public Goods [2]

Historically, air and water have not been privately owned. The explanation of this situation lies in the difficulty or impossibility of excluding people from the use of these resources and in the fact that, until recently, both resources have appeared to be available in an unlimited supply. There has been no profit incentive to claim ownership of air and water and charge for their use. In the case of air, exclusion and a user charge would be impossible. With water these possibilities exist, but attempting to exclude people from the use of a water body usually is too expensive in relation to the potential revenue. Air and most large bodies of water have become, de facto, commonly owned. Their use has been permitted without price payments on a first-come-first-served basis. The river has been used for recreation until a municipality or industry pre-empts its use. In addition to sustaining life, air serves as a waste receptor for automobile and power plant emissions. The social value of these pre-emptive reallocations cannot be determined because the ownership of air and water has not been legally defined. When goods are sold for a price (and all the assumptions of perfect competition are met), the presumption is that the resources used in producing those goods are correctly allocated. When goods, such as air and water, are not sold, the presumption of correct allocation cannot be made.

Legally defined ownership would not in itself solve the problem. The nature of common property resources is such that large numbers of people and firms may use them simultaneously when they have been allocated to a given use. As a consequence, individual decisions with respect to the use of such resources may not be socially correct. For example, all would benefit from cleaner air. Each individual might be willing to pay a price — say, $10 a month — in order to have clean air, but we may not be willing to offer automobile producers an extra $120 a year in order to obtain cleaner air.

Is your valuation of cleaner air equal to the extra cost of lead-free automobile gasoline? If your monthly dollar valuation of cleaner air is equal to, or greater than, the added cost per month of lead-free gas (including decreased "performance" and the time it takes you to drive to a station that sells lead-free gas) and you choose not to buy it, your behavior illustrates the way rational consumers can fail to produce socially optimal results. If you were asked to justify your antisocial behavior, you would probably use the following argument: if I buy lead-free gas and no one else does, then the air is really not going to be cleaner; on the other hand, if everyone else buys lead-free gas, the air will be cleaner and I will not have to buy lead-free gas. Obviously, if everyone follows the same line of reasoning, no one will make the socially correct choice. Your argument is not unreasonable. Your reasoning is applicable to a whole range of "public goods." Whenever a good is consumed jointly by more than one person, it becomes, for analytical purposes, a public good. Some instances of public goods are trivial to the overall performance of the economy; others are not. If you share a dormitory room with another person, the room is a public good. The deterrent effect of military spending and the legal system are public goods. The common characteristic of these goods is joint consumption. Once produced, they are equally available to all. Their use by one person does not detract from their use by another person. The joint consumption aspect of public goods accounts for the "free rider" phenomenon. Specifically, if everyone else buys lead-free gas, you do not have to buy it to obtain cleaner air. When you can be a "free rider," you will not volunteer a contribution.

The other aspect of this line of reasoning is not as easily explained. Under what circumstances will a consumer make a voluntary payment for a public good even though the free riders will not pay? Basically, the consumer will buy the public good when his enjoyment of the good outweighs his reluctance to benefit free riders. For example, I may detest mosquitoes enough to have the swamp in back of my home sprayed even though my neighbors will benefit and refuse to share the cost. That is to say, the gain I expect to receive may exceed the cost of producing benefits for myself as well as for others. With most important cases of public goods, however, the first unit of the good is so expensive that no one person will be able or willing to assume the cost. No one person's contribution is sufficient to produce the first unit of defense deterrence. One person's purchase of lead-free gas will simply not be sufficient to produce noticeably cleaner air. The amount that one person might be willing to pay to produce a cleaner river will not be sufficient to make a difference in water quality. The sum of the contributions of all persons, however, may be sufficient to call forth a noticeable improvement in water quality. If the sum of contributions is sufficient to improve the river and the river remains polluted, the market system has failed to produce the correct social choice — a decrease in the consumption of other goods and an increase in the quality of the water.

There are then, two problems associated with public goods. First, since these goods cannot be parceled out in discrete units in response to price bids, aggregation of payments to cover costs of production does not occur. Second, each person has the incentive to let other people pay for his benefits. The net effect of these characteristics of public goods is that such goods are not likely to be produced in socially correct amounts unless people force themselves — through government — to make payments they would otherwise withhold. Thus, the production of public goods such as pollution abatement becomes a matter of social — as opposed to individual — choice.

The Problem of Social Choice

The environmental problem, as has been indicated, arises from the failure of the market system to measure the value which people attach to cleaner air and water and its failure to force the consideration of that value when decisions are made about alternative uses of air and water. The first task of government is to discover the extent to which people value cleaner air and water and to compare the citizen's willingness to pay for abatement with the cost of abatement. In short, we must rely on the political mechanism to do what the market fails to do: set standards of air and water quality. The next task of government is to design and carry out programs to insure that such standards are met in practice.

The nature of the policy-making task and some of the obstacles to the formulation of correct environmental standards can be illustrated with a simple example. First, however, a criterion for the correctness of resource allocation decisions — including those relating to standards of environmental quality — must be specified.

The Economic Efficiency Criterion   The usefulness of the market allocation technique and, alternatively, of political decision-making tools, can be judged only with reference to an agreed upon criterion. If someone were to ask you if the United States Government were performing well, your answer would reflect your own preferences relative to government outputs and your share of their tax costs. Eco-

nomic theory invokes a more general criterion of performance —
everyone's welfare as judged by each person's preferences.

The phrase "everyone's welfare" needs a precise definition.
Assume a group of only two people. Most people would agree that
the well-being of that group is improved or increased when both of
them have more goods than they had initially. If someone gave you
and a friend a free case of soda and a free case of beer each week,
you would both feel that your welfare had been improved. Economic
theory goes a step further and concludes that the welfare of you and
your friend, as a society, is improved if either one of you has more
goods available to him, as long as the other one does not have fewer
goods. More generally, whenever the welfare of one person is increased without decreasing the welfare of someone else, the efficiency criterion used by many economists would conclude that the
society has experienced an increase in total welfare. This criterion
makes sense only when we assume that a person's feeling of well-
being depends only on his absolute level of income and not on his income position relative to others. Even when a person's income is not
decreased he may well feel worse off if the incomes of others are increasing.

The economic efficiency criterion does not permit direct judgments
of the effectiveness of either the private or the public sector. The criterion yields no insight into the most pressing of society's problems
— those concerned with the distribution of goods among the members of the society. For example, the criterion cannot be used to
judge whether wealth should be transferred from the very wealthy to
the destitute. This transfer would improve the welfare of one group at
the expense of another. The economic efficiency criterion says nothing about whether such a redistribution would be good or bad. In addition, the objective observer of the economy's performance lacks
knowledge of people's preferences. The analyst can only examine
various types of decision-making institutions and question whether
they are likely to yield solutions conforming to individual preferences.

A Simple Problem of Social Choice [3]   A hypothetical example, which
raises the same problems that arise regarding the proper use of
water and air, illustrates the nature of the decision-making problems
associated with allocating resources to the production of public
goods. There are three homes lined up along a road. In the back, on
a set of vacant lots, is a surface water pond in which mosquitos
breed. The mosquitoes are viewed as a nuisance by the residents of
the three houses. What is the socially "correct" level of mosquito
control? Will that level be achieved through voluntary, atomistic be-

havior? Will any kind of nonmarket decision-making device select the correct solution? The measurement problem is assumed away by "making up" data and it is assumed that all three persons have the same income and share identical attitudes toward the value of mosquito control as opposed to other goods. Units of mosquito control are defined as each consisting of a ten percent reduction of the original total. The willingness of each person to pay is assumed to be represented by the following marginal valuation schedule.

Units of Control	Marginal Valuation	Marginal Cost
1	$10/month	$6/month
2	9	6
3	8	6
4	7	6
5	6	6
6	5	6
7	4	6
8	3	6
9	2	6
10	1	6

The marginal cost of mosquito control is assumed constant at six dollars per unit. Under these circumstances, it is in the interest of any one of the individuals to purchase up to five units of control. Up to the fifth unit, any one of the three persons is willing to pay for the extra unit because it costs him less than it is worth. Suppose that one of the three persons is impulsive and makes the decision to purchase five units of control. After this decision is made, will any further change in the three parties' relative purchases of mosquito control and other goods improve the welfare of at least one of the three without lowering any one else's welfare. If such a change were possible, the welfare of the whole group could be improved. Given the way this example has been set up, an improvement would be possible. No one places a high enough value on the sixth unit to pay the six dollar cost. However, sharing the cost of the sixth unit among the three could reduce each person's marginal payment below his marginal valuation. For example, if the three persons agreed to divide the cost of the sixth unit equally, each could obtain added benefits which he considers to be worth five dollars for a contribution of only two dollars. All three persons can gain from cooperative cost sharing. Gains from cost sharing will be possible up to the ninth unit of control. For the ninth unit, the sum of the three persons' marginal valuations of mosquito control exactly equals the marginal cost. Beyond the ninth unit, given an equal distribution of marginal costs, each person would have to pay more than his one dollar marginal valuation. Hence, given our assumptions, nine units is the socially correct level of output of mosquito control, with the marginal cost divided equally among all parties.

Two major points may be illustrated with the above example. First, in the absence of cooperative action among the three individuals, a less than optimal amount of mosquito control will be produced because the marginal cost of producing more than five units is in excess of each person's marginal valuation. Second, it is in the interest of each of the three parties to purchase at least five units of the good for his own benefit.

The result in the example, however, may be somewhat unrealistic. The marginal cost of mosquito control may be unrealistically low in this example. Assuming that the marginal valuation schedule is the same and that each unit of mosquito control costs twenty-four dollars, no one would purchase the first unit. Mosquito control, in this case of high unit cost, has both of the characteristics of a public good that were mentioned above: a marginal cost in excess of the marginal valuation and the "free-rider" phenomenon. Even though the optimal level of production would be three units (where the sum of the marginal valuations exactly equals marginal cost), none of the good would be purchased.

Two of the initial questions have been answered. A socially optimal level of output for the public good is that level at which the sum of the marginal valuations of all members of a society equals the marginal cost. The optimal level of output will not necessarily be attained through individual — as opposed to group — behavior.

Will cooperative action yield through group decision-making the correct solution? Suppose that in the context of the six-dollar marginal cost, one person has purchased five units and all three people, recognizing the benefits from collective action, get together to decide on whether to purchase the sixth unit. Assume that each person will agree to the purchase of an added unit and share the added cost as long as he is not harmed. In this circumstance, each individual would be willing to pay up to five dollars for an additional unit. If individual A paid five dollars, then B and C would have to share only the remaining one dollar of the six dollar marginal cost. The same would be true of A and B if C paid five dollars. Will any one of the three admit to his true marginal valuation of the sixth unit? Perhaps each person, hoping that the others will contribute enough to cover marginal cost, will initially not admit to a marginal valuation greater than zero. When it is recognized that the understated marginal valuations do not add up to the full marginal cost and that no one will receive the benefits of the added unit, each participant in the bargaining process will increase his offer. Eventually a bargain will be struck which will be satisfactory to all of the parties involved and added units of control will be purchased. Group decision-making, when only a few parties are involved, has the potential for yielding gains for all parties through cost-sharing.

The problem of arriving at an optimal agreement is compounded if the marginal valuation schedules for the three parties differ; but in principle the potential for agreement on output levels and cost shares still exists.

The decision problem becomes intractable when large numbers of persons are involved. The cost of communication between affected parties becomes larger, perhaps out of proportion to the increase in numbers of persons, and the influence of the "free-rider" effect inhibits the movement toward an optimal level of output. In the case of a small number of people, the contribution of each is a substantial share of marginal cost and a participant who fails to reveal his marginal valuation is able to see his potential welfare loss. When large numbers of people are involved, the connection between the payment volunteered and the amount of benefits received loses its immediacy. No one will feel that his own failure to contribute will reduce the output sufficiently to lower noticeably his benefits. If your payment for defense spending were voluntary and you valued deterrence at ten dollars per year, you would recognize that if you volunteered only five dollars, the total amount of deterrence produced would not be materially changed. If everyone were to reason this way, the iterative process of adjusting voluntary contributions upward toward true marginal valuation would necessitate a costly and time-consuming trial-and-error learning process.

Despite its simplicity, this model of social choice is not without practical value. The reader might ask himself why neighbors do not negotiate to share the cost of tree planting, lawn maintenance, or house painting. Each of these expenditures provides joint consumption benefits as well as benefits to the single purchaser. Cost-sharing might be mutually beneficial in any one of these activities; but the costs of reaching a mutually beneficial decision on sharing the costs of such expenditures are apparently too high relative to the expected gain.

The model has even broader normative and descriptive significance. As a descriptive theory, the model provides one explanation of why people choose to tax themselves through government. In effect, the coercive power of government in forcing people to make payments for publicly produced goods is used as a substitute for the coercive power of a private property market system. Since pollution abatement clearly provides benefits which are in the nature of public goods — benefits which are jointly consumed — decisions about the production of pollution abatement are necessarily governmental decisions. The public nature of pollution abatement explains government concern with it. If we did not turn to government for pollution abatement, the benefits of cleaner air and water would likely be foregone.

The public goods model also provides an idealized decision-making framework within which water and air quality standard-setting may be conceptualized. Pollution abatement is not unlike mosquito control; it is costly and is jointly consumed. If society is concerned with efficiency, choices among alternative uses of common property resources require a balancing of marginal benefits and costs. At the highest level of aggregation the model requires that reductions in air and water pollution continue as long as the sum of everyone's marginal valuations of cleaner air and water is greater than the marginal cost of abating pollution. In the above example, marginal valuations are revealed through a simple process of reaching an agreement on whether an extra expenditure on mosquito control should be made. In the real world, perhaps because of the high costs of informal decision-making, more structured processes are used.

Alternative Policy-Making Techniques for Making Social Choices

Policy decisions about the use of common property resources — that is, decisions about the extent to which such resources will be used as waste-receptors or for other purposes — could be made in a variety of ways. At one extreme, society could rely totally on a central decision-maker. This "dictatorship" model is judged to be so unlikely to yield socially correct decisions that it is not worth considering. At the other extreme, total reliance could be placed on direct popular voting through referenda. In the middle, mixed decision-making systems relying on representative bodies and executive agencies may be used. In the following section some of the major obstacles to efficient social choice will be examined in the context of the referendum technique. The difficulties illustrated with reference to referenda will also be present in the mixed system which is characteristic of current American social choice processes.

Benefit-Cost Analysis   Optimization of pollution abatement can be seen as a comparison of social marginal valuation with social marginal costs. Since this is so, an objective analysis should be able to compute the best level of abatement of a given pollutant by calculating and comparing marginal costs and benefits. Benefit-cost analysis — a decision-making tool which has gained currency primarily in the analysis of water resource investments — provides the vehicle for making such comparisons. Conceptually, such an analysis of pollution abatement would be straightforward. For a specific pollutant of a specific receptor — for example, biochemical oxygen demand in a particular stretch of river — the analyst might wish to calculate the cost of obtaining successive improvements in water quality and compare this cost to calculated dollar measures of benefits derived from successive increments of water quality. The best level of abatement would be that at which the total difference between benefits and costs is greatest or, what amounts to the same thing, that level at which increasing or constant marginal cost equals decreasing marginal benefit. In practice, this kind of analysis is not particularly compelling in making abatement policy. The central difficulty of carrying out the analysis is that the more important benefits of pollution abatement, in the case of both air and water, cannot be subjected to dollar measurement. Although one might come up with fairly good estimates of the value of shellfish destroyed as a result of water pollution, one would be hard-pressed to place a dollar value on most recreational uses of a river or on the esthetic and psychological values of clean water. In the absence of accurate means of measurement, the benefits are likely to be understated. Perhaps as a result of the uncertainty attaching to benefit-cost estimates, we have relied on political decision-making techniques to make environmental policy.

Majority Versus Unanimity Rule From the economist's point of view, people's voting behavior is influenced by their evaluation of the benefits and costs resulting from each possible outcome. If you were asked to vote on whether the automobile industry should be required to produce cars with no carbon monoxide emissions, you would want to know how emission reductions would benefit you and also how much the decision to require auto emissions free from carbon monoxide would cost you. If your subjective evaluation of your expected benefits were greater than your expected costs, you would vote in favor of the proposal; if not, you would vote against it. Whether social decisions made on this basis would be correct in terms of the ideal model described above depends on, among other things, the rule used to determine whether a proposal is accepted or rejected.

Generally a simple majority vote will not produce the socially correct decision. A socially correct allocation of resources is one in which each and every person cannot improve his sense of well-being by giving up some goods and using the released money to purchase another good. When majority rule obtains and the majority is less than 100 percent, the above criterion will be violated. Some individuals will feel that they are paying too much for the benefits they receive from the public good; they would prefer to "spend" less on the public good and buy more of some private goods or some other public good. Conversely, some people will feel they are paying too little and would be willing to pay more for the amount of benefits they receive from the public good. In effect, the former group will be experiencing an involuntary loss in welfare, while the latter group will be experiencing an involuntary gain. It is important to note that this problem will not arise in the case of private goods. A person must make a payment for a private good and will adjust his consumption so that he would experience no net gain by buying less of that good and more of something else. In the case of a public good, individuals do not have this option. Hence, it is clear that using the simple majority rule permits nonoptimal policy choices to be made and to persist.

The Full Employment Assumption   In moving from an idealized referendum to real world voting situations, obstacles to socially correct decisions multiply. The welfare model underlying the economist's conjectures about voting behavior diverges radically from the reality of the market economy. Statements defining the socially correct allocation of resources and analyses of the various nonmarket techniques of making resource allocation decisions always, at least implicitly, assume full employment of resources. Thus, if a vote were taken on the advisability of expanding or contracting space explorations, each person would be expected to make his decision on the basis of his personal evaluation of the product involved (increased scientific knowledge, higher national prestige, entertaining television coverage) relative to his estimation of his share of the cost. A space technologist would naturally tend to vote in favor of expanding space appropriations not because he necessarily valued the space program's output per se but simply because he earned income from this program. His vote provides him with some influence over the demand for his product. In the economist's ideal model of perfect competition this purely monetary consideration would be irrelevant. With perfect resource mobility the demand for one's own product would not influence one's rate of return as a productive agent. If resources were perfectly mobile, a cut in the space program would not decrease the income of workers in the program. If one lost one's job, one would be instantly reemployed doing something else. Clearly, a worker would then be in a position to vote for or against the space budget only on the basis of its tax costs to him and his honest evaluation of the worth of further space exploration.

Obviously such a model is unreal. Resource transfers are not without cost. Unemployment resulting from declining demand or from technological change can be of long duration. Recognizing this fact, people will take every opportunity to make sure that external influences do not lead to a loss of jobs. The shoe factory workers and the shoe factory owners will favor protective tariff legislation. Contractors and automobile producers will favor the construction of roads. Teachers will support education bond issues. Economists will support the institutionalization of economic analysis.

If all governmental expenditure decisions were made by referenda, people's concern for loss of jobs would perhaps not be of great significance. Assume that the decision on continued use of Federal funds to develop an SST (supersonic transport) were to have been made through a nationwide referendum. Also assume that development costs would have been divided equally among voters and that the majority rule applied. If voters looked only at the direct (nonmonetary) benefits stemming from the program, those who felt that their benefits were less than their costs would vote "no" and those who felt direct benefits exceeded costs would vote "yes." Suppose that if votes were cast only on this basis, the "yes" votes were a 55-percent majority. The decision would be reversed if 6 percent of the voters worked in the aerospace industry and would have voted "no" except for the fact that they expected monetary benefits.

Consideration of monetary benefits would become decisive in influencing the outcome of a referendum only in those cases in which sufficient "no" votes are changed to "yes" votes to yield a majority of "yes" votes. Obviously, the larger the expenditure under consideration and the larger the number of people for whom the program creates employment, the more important this consideration becomes. In most cases, there will not be enough monetary beneficiaries from government spending programs to influence the outcome of a referendum.

The type of phenomenon described above will be of considerable importance in the making of pollution control decisions. The production of some products will be curtailed because of decreases in quantity demanded as prices rise to reflect pollution control costs. Owners of physical and human capital in affected industries and in industries supplying affected industries stand to lose income.

Conversely, it should be expected that certain pecuniary interests will favor pollution control expenditures. Producers of waste treatment facilities and those trained in their operation (as well as those who are employed in training them) will likely favor expanded pollution abatement efforts. Those who produce products which are substitutes for pollution-producing goods will also gain from pollution control.

The Perception of Benefits and Costs   The model of voter behavior requires that each voter be able at least to estimate his marginal cost and his benefits. This requirement is very restrictive. Most voters are fairly uncertain about their personal gains from a given expenditure. Only in the case of gross differentials in the incidence of benefits will the voter be able to estimate the effects of an expenditure. Local education bond issues are a case in point. Older couples whose children (if any) have already finished school will see little merit in a new high school building. While they may vote for the bond issue out of altruism, they will clearly not do so out of self-interest (except perhaps to the extent that they feel that better buildings mean better education and better education will produce a better citizenry and better neighbors). On the other hand, the couple with four children in elementary school would clearly stand to benefit from a new high school. If the cost share from the expenditure were the same for both couples, the latter would probably vote for, and the former against, the bond issue.

Usually the voter's ability to estimate the benefits to be received from pollution abatement expenditures is limited. The individual voter simply does not know the degree of improvement in water quality which will result from a municipal waste treatment bond issue. Most voters probably assume that a given expenditure will produce *some* benefit. If the costs are not "too high," they vote for the goal of cleaner water and assume that the program will yield progress toward meeting that goal. The voter's knowledge of the correctness of the decision comes only after the expenditure is made.

Uncertainty about the outcome of expenditure programs leaves an informational vacuum. The vacuum is filled in part by the bureaucrats responsible for designing effective programs. Just as the consumer must place some trust in the manufacturer of a television set, he has to place similar trust in the designers of public programs. The vacuum is also filled, in part, by program advocates. Not surprisingly, those who stand to benefit monetarily will seek to display that program in a favorable light.

Even if a voter can estimate his expected benefits, he must also be able to estimate his share of the cost. While cost shares can be determined objectively in theory, in practice a variety of considerations

introduce uncertainty into the voter's cost estimates. Consider the
A.B.C. Paper Co., Inc. The mill emits unpleasant odors over an area
roughly congruent with its labor market. The question before the voters in the affected area is whether the plant should be required to install the appropriate devices to totally eliminate odors. The incidence
of costs, and people's guesses about the incidence of costs, will vary
radically with different methods of financing.

If the firm has to finance its own pollution control expenditures, the
mechanisms of the price system will determine the distribution of the
costs. The major problem facing the voter will be the impact of these
costs on his income. If he is employed by the polluting firm, there is
the possibility of unemployment. If his income is derived from selling
goods to the firm or its employees, his income is endangered. The
firm's reaction to the controls can range from accepting a profit reduction and maintaining a constant output to complete shutdown.

If pollution control decisions were made through referenda with the
real cost of abatement programs assigned to voters indirectly
through the price mechanism, the typical voter would be unable to
determine his share of the cost and would be uncertain about his employment. The information gap would be filled by those who felt
strongly about the consequences of the decision. Public decisions
made on such tenuous grounds are not likely to be optimal. Indeed,
fears of unemployment and loss of profits in particular polluting industries are likely to bias decisions in favor of less than optimal commitments to cleaner air and water.

The voter may have the alternative of financing the full cost of
abatement through the public budget. The burden which each taxpayer will have to bear depends, then, on the type of tax which is increased to cover the cost of subsidies. If the cleanup program is
financed at the Federal level, the necessary revenues would probably
be raised from personal and corporate income taxes. Each person's
share would then depend on his income tax bracket and upon the extent to which corporate taxes are shifted forward to consumers,
backward to workers, or absorbed out of corporate profits. If the
cleanup program is financed on the state level, the incidence of costs
will depend on which state tax is increased. If a general sales tax is
increased, the incidence of costs will be regressive (that is, the increased tax payment as a percent of income will be larger for the
lower income taxpayer than for the higher income taxpayer). If a
state income tax is increased, the incidence will depend on the rate
structure and, again, on the ability of corporations to shift the burden
of higher taxes forward or backward. If the program is to be financed
locally, in most areas the property tax would then be on owner-occu-

pants or residential properties, on renters, and on consumers in general as a major portion of the property tax is generally thought to be shifted forward. In any case, it will be difficult for the individual taxpayer to forecast his share of the cost of governmentally financed pollution abatement.

Perhaps the most important distinction between direct and indirect financing techniques is that the former do not entail employment losses in the polluting industries. When governments raise revenues at near full employment levels of national income, people are forced to buy fewer privately produced goods. The resulting employment losses are widely diffused so that no single group of firms or workers feels directly threatened and the fear of employment losses is effectively neutralized as an influence on political decisions. Hence, direct government financing of pollution abatement might well increase the likelihood of optimal decisions. Economists would argue strenuously, however, that indirect financing techniques are superior to direct government subsidies. The correct use of resources requires that the full cost of producing each good be reflected in its price. If some production processes interfere with alternative uses of common property resources, the cost of reducing that interference to a socially acceptable level should be reflected in the prices of products produced by those processes. The consumer could then decide whether to pay the higher price or shift to other goods.

Reliance on indirect financing requires social policies aimed at eliminating from consideration possible employment losses from pollution control decisions. Until such policies are designed and implemented, there is little hope that voter responses to pollution control policy decisions will reflect the true costs of alternatives.

Given voter uncertainties regarding the costs and benefits, referenda are, not surprisingly, used infrequently in making governmental allocation decisions. Some specialization of the decision-making function is clearly useful in terms of improving the efficiency of the gathering, dissemination, and evaluation of information. Representative decision-making systems are meant to provide this specialization and efficiency. Unfortunately, as we shall see, such systems are at least equally susceptible to bias and error as are referenda.

Representative Decision-Making Systems While the realities of political decision-making bear little surface resemblance to the structure of the economic model of voters weighing costs against benefits, the basic processes are quite similar and the bias resulting from fears of unemployment and profit losses are no less important.

The costliness of referenda is avoided by the use of representative

bodies. While the net benefit of substituting representative government for "town meeting" government can be evaluated only with reference to the ability of each to promote "correct" social decisions, in
a technical sense representative government is the less costly approach. Decisions, like goods and services, can be produced in more
or less costly ways. Obviously, if each individual in the United States
had to assess the personal costs and benefits of every government
decision, he would have little time to do anything else. The voter ex-
pects his representative to the city council, state assembly, or Congress to be informed about the consequences of each decision and
to reflect the voter's interests. If nothing else, specialization in the
collection of information yields substantial economies.

Economies in the communication of information about preferences
are also obtained through representative government. Reducing the
number of participants in the actual voting process reduces the cost
of summing up their preferences on a given issue. The repetitive process of evaluating outcomes of past decisions and altering commitments of resources requires a constant flow of information back to
policy-makers and a constant process of incorporating new information into new decisions.

Federal Policy-Making and Budgeting Process

The full complexity and limitations of representative decision-making
processes in an advanced economy can be seen in the system
through which public resource allocation decisions are made in the
United States. Resource allocation policy-making at the Federal level
involves two fairly distinct stages. The first stage is the decision to
enter an entirely new field of operations, and the second stage entails
subsequent annual decisions on expanding or contracting financial
commitments in a given area. Decisions to enter a new field are
made fairly infrequently. Beginning a large-scale highway grant program, a medical insurance program, or a broadly based attack on
poverty or environmental problems requires either a reordering of
spending priorities within a given budget or an increase in tax payments (when the economy is near full employment). Consequently,
such programs require either widespread public support (whether
innate or induced by those who are in a position to influence public
attitudes) or sufficient direct pressure on decision-makers.

While the action of Congress and the signature of the President
establish a program, funds must be appropriated by the Congress
before agencies can incur spending obligations. The second stage in
the policy-making system — the process of budgeting — then begins.

Most appropriations are reviewed annually. Executive agencies submit their budget requests to the President. The President's budget staff, the Office of Management and Budget, reviews agencies' requests in light of the President's priorities and in the context of the total budget's impact on aggregate demand. The budget submitted by the President goes first to the House Committee on Appropriations and is subdivided into elements to be considered separately by the relevant subcommittees. The subcommittees hold hearings at which the agencies are expected to justify their requests. When the subcommittee's adjustments have been made, the subcommittee returns its share of the budget to the full committee. The full committee usually approves the subcommittee's report. The full House then acts on each major segment of the budget. A similar sequence then takes place in the Senate. If the House and Senate bills differ — as they usually do — differences are worked out in a Conference Committee. Each major appropriations bill then goes to the President who can accept or veto the entire bill (not its specific components). While the President generally cannot spend more on a program than is appropriated by Congress, he can choose to spend less.

Describing the structure of the budgeting process reveals little about the likelihood of its producing "correct" social policy decisions. Perhaps the most outstanding characteristics of the process are its "fragmented" and "incremental" nature.[4] While the executive is capable of taking a global view of the budget, Congressional opportunities for making major decisions on spending priorities are severely restricted. In the past, the full House and Senate have tended to accept the decisions of the appropriations subcommittees. In recent years, intense Senate debates have focused on matters of "national priorities." The Senate debates over funding the antiballistic missile program and the supersonic transport indicate the problems of the budgeting process. The time and effort involved is so great that the number of substantive issues which can be subject to complete review in a given year is severely limited. Furthermore, in recent years, partly as the result of the depth to which the ABM and SST issues have been examined, it has been well into the fiscal year before the relevant budget has reached the President's desk. Thus, centralized Congressional evaluation of policy issues is infrequent, and policy decisions are assigned to committees and subcommittees. When issues of national priorities are dealt with in depth, the budgetary process is disrupted. It is not surprising, then, that budget decisions are made in a fragmented, decentralized way.

The Federal allocation process may also be termed "incremental." The Federal budget is not created from scratch every year. Agencies try to justify, and Congress reviews, incremental increases in spending levels.[5]

Some students of the budgeting process have argued strenuously that fragmentation and incrementalism are essential to the effectiveness of Federal decision-making.[6] Fragmentation has the advantage of reducing to manageable proportions the exceedingly complex budget document. An appropriations subcommittee can develop a reasonably high level of expertise in a given functional area. Fragmentation is reputed to have the added advantage of allowing decision-makers to ignore values that may be held by other affected persons. The agency's budget staff need not consider the "general welfare"; they know that if their decisions adversely affect a particular interest group, that group will have its supporters elsewhere.

Those who favor the incremental approach emphasize that decision-making is a learning process. Lindblom has argued that the weight society attaches to various goals can only be known after steps have been taken toward their accomplishment.[7] The nation's tolerance for inflation, for example, will only be known when the level of unemployment associated with a given rate of inflation is also known. The Vietnam war is a classic example of this phenomenon. The lack of social tolerance for foregoing private and public consumption and for loss of lives was not foreseen by decision-makers. Intolerance of rising deaths and casualties and of domestic inflation became clear only after the nation had experienced them.

While fragmentation and incrementalism may be necessary for practical reasons, they have elements which contribute to distorted policy decisions. Fragmentation places a great deal of power in the hands of a few people who are politically responsible only to a limited constituency. Special interest group lobbying is likely to be more effective (and obviously is less expensive) if only a small number of decision-makers must be influenced. Industry and labor groups which anticipate losses or gains in profits or employment from a specific policy decision can easily bring lobbying pressure to bear. Thus, a decision to expand the ABM system will reflect the influence of both those who feel that an expansion is desirable per se and those who expect to earn money and maintain employment in researching, developing, and producing the system. Likewise, decisions about pollution abatement will reflect the influence of potential monetary beneficiaries and losers. The majority of citizens who are concerned only with the real costs and benefits from a decision are simply not organized to exercise countervailing power.

The force of pecuniary interest groups is especially strong when attempts are made to contract a program's funding level or alter its structural characteristics. When the Defense Department attempts to close down redundant military bases, opposition from Congressmen whose local districts are affected presents a major political obstacle. If the affected Congressmen enjoy the prerogatives of seniority, it is very difficult to get the bases closed. Similarly, cutting back on the space program has proved difficult in the face of unemployment in the aerospace industry. These considerations, from an efficiency point of view, should be irrelevant. The existence of constituencies for large scale public spending programs produces a great deal of inertia in the decision-making process. Any new efforts in the environmental area will face special interest group opposition from both those expecting monetary losses from the program and those seeking to maintain or expand the level of funding in competing governmental programs.

Total reliance on incrementalism also heightens the risks of having to endure adverse program consequences that might have been predicted and evaluated beforehand. Lindblom presents a hypothetical example of a greatly expanded highway program designed for national defense, economic growth, and a reduction in highway congestion.[8] In Lindblom's example, the effects of the program on the location of economic activity and the rate of use of natural resources are ignored. According to Lindblom these consequences *should* be ignored since they can neither be predicted with any degree of accuracy nor be evaluated until they actually occur. The construction of the United States' interstate highway system bears a remarkable resemblance to Lindblom's example. In retrospect, it would have been useful to know the environmental consequences of the program. Whether these consequences could have been known in advance is a moot question. The Vietnam war, another triumph of incrementalism, also illustrates the additional possibility that supporters of a program can sometimes postpone its consequences. Most economists would prefer to see a larger dose of a priori analysis of possible program outputs and costs than is currently carried out at the Federal level.

The conclusions to be drawn from the preceding discussion are that public decision-making is a sequential, marginal process relying on program evaluation after the program is established and that a great deal of inertia characterizes the process because vested interests resist contraction of ongoing programs and thus limit the funding of new programs. Both of these processes have played and will continue to play important roles in the evolution of Federal pollution control legislation. Pollution abatement will be costly, and expectations about the magnitude and the distribution of costs have influenced and will continue to influence the formulation of pollution control programs.

Budgeting for Environmental Improvement

A review of the extent to which environmental programs have been funded in the Federal budget suggests that the financial commitment has been relatively small. Federal outlays for environmental improvement are included in a broad category described as "natural resources and environment." The category encompasses expenditures for pollution control and abatement, recreational resources such as natural and historical sites, water resources projects including navigation and irrigation projects by the Corps of Engineers and Bureau of Reclamation, land management, and mineral research projects such as coal gasification.

The total outlays for the natural resources and environmental category are listed in Table 8-1. In terms of total budget outlays, expenditures for natural resources and environment represent a rather small amount. The table, however, does not adequately reflect the extent of Federal funding of environmental improvement programs. While all

Table 8-1 Federal Budget Outlays for Natural Resources and Environment

Fiscal year	Total outlays (millions of dollars)	Percentage of total budget outlays (%)	Pollution control and abatement expenditures as a percentage of total outlays for natural resources and environment
1973 (est.)	$2,450	1.0	62.9*
1972 (est.)	4,376	1.8	29.4
1971	2,716	1.3	25.8
1970	2,480	1.3	13.6
1969	2,081	1.1	14.0
1968	1,655	0.9	14.5
1967	1,821	1.2	10.1
1966	1,999	1.5	7.8
1965	2,028	1.7	6.5
1964	1,944	1.7	6.9
1963	1,483	1.3	5.8
1962	1,665	1.6	n.a.

Source: Executive Office of the President, Office of Management and Budget, *The U.S. Budget in Brief, 1973* (Washington: United States Government Printing Office, 1972), pp. 53 and 79.
* This figure is unrepresentative of past outlays because total 1973 outlays for natural resources and environment are only 50 percent of the 1972 level due to an abnormally large inflow of offsetting receipts from the sale of oil and gas leases and mineral leases. The increase mainly occurs due to a Supreme Court order requiring distribution of receipts from oil and gas lease sales previously held in escrow due to a dispute over state boundaries. (Source: The Budget of the U.S. Government, 1973, pp. 107–108.)

the programs included in the broad category have some role in a general environmental policy, perhaps the most important category of expenditures is pollution control and abatement. These outlays, expressed as a percent of total expenditures for natural resources and environmental programs, are presented in Table 8-1. The table shows the heavy and increasing commitment of dollars to programs for abatement and control. Actual expenditures for abatement and control in 1967 represented only 10.1 percent of the total but by 1971 actual outlays equalled 25.8 percent of the total.

The expenditures for various environmental programs listed in Table 8-1 are not all attributable to the Environmental Protection Agency. Prior to the creation of EPA, major responsibilities for Federal environmental policy were scattered throughout five separate Federal agencies. With the creation of the EPA, major responsibility was centralized in one agency. This change was obviously necessary to develop a unified and consistent policy. In spite of this centralization, some elements of the earlier situation remain. The major Federal agencies with environmental responsibilities are listed in Table 8-2.

In terms of dollar outlays for pollution control, the EPA is by far the most important agency. The figures in Table 8-2 should be interpreted with caution. A small expenditure does not necessarily mean

Table 8-2   Pollution Control and Abatement Activities, by Agency
(Millions of Dollars)

	1971 Actual	1972 Estimate	1973 Estimate
Environmental Protection Agency	$718	$1,287	$1,544
Defense, Military	82	130	235
Atomic Energy Commission	122	136	154
Transportation	22	56	79
Agriculture	67	107	139
Defense, Civil	7	50	56
Interior	45	87	82
Commerce	20	26	30
General Service Administration	2	2	5
National Aeronautics and Space Administration	25	30	29
National Science Foundation	9	11	15
Other agencies	31	53	72
Total	1,149	1,975	2,440

Source: *The Budget of the United States Government—Special Analysis* (Washington: United States Government Printing Office, 1972), p. 298.

that an agency plays a minor role in formulating Federal environmental policy. This warning would certainly apply in the case of the Atomic Energy Commission, which is concerned with formulating policy to control the environmental impact of nuclear generating plants. The allocation of funds to various environmental programs is covered in the following chapter, which considers the development of air and water pollution control legislation.

9

The History of Federal Environmental Legislation

The political-economic model of public decision-making in Chapter 8 indicates that environmental legislation must consider three distinct problems. First, the policy-making task must be assigned to an appropriate institution — whether legislative or administrative, whether local, state, or Federal. Second, standards for performance must be designed and implemented. Third, the programs, plans, and mechanisms must, in time, result in measurable progress towards the goal. Analysis indicates that none of these problems has yet been solved.

Water Pollution Control

A national environmental policy which recognizes the trade-offs between waste-receptor and clean water uses continues to evolve as production technology, pollution control technology, and public water-use preferences change. The evolution is taking place in the disjointed manner suggested by the incrementalist analysis of public decision-making. The legislative process has responded in an incremental fashion to pressures from vested interest groups, environmentalists, and the cost-benefit feedback from past experiences.

Only recently has the importance of explicitly recognizing waste receptor/clean use trade-offs been appreciated and given status in

Federal law. The history of environmental legislation has been characterized by indecisive commitments to environmental goals, underfunding of existing programs, and experimentation with alternative program designs and policy-making techniques.

Early Environmental Legislation   Early legislation relating to current environmental problems reflected concern with only a subset of non-waste-receptor uses of water bodies.[1] Perhaps the earliest instance of Federal environmental legislation arose from the conflict between waste disposal and navigation. The Rivers and Harbors Act of 1890 prohibited the dumping of wastes in navigable waters when dumping would interfere with navigation.[2] The Act was superseded by Section 13 of the Rivers and Harbors Act of 1899. This latter act included a blanket prohibition — apparently irrespective of possible interference with navigation — of waste disposal into navigable waters. Exceptions could be permitted by the Secretary of War.[3] Section 13, known as the Refuse Act of 1899, was moribund until its 1970 revival by environmental activists. Ralph Nader's task force on water pollution reported that during the law's seventy year history only four Section 13 permits were issued by the Army Corps of Engineers; yet, between 1899 and 1969, the number of point sources of industrial water pollution had risen to about 40,000.[4] Although the Act's provisions had been used in some specific instances,[5] until 1969 the law had not been used to pursue the broader goals of environmental protection. The "rediscovery" and recent history of the Refuse Act will be discussed below.

The second narrowly focused water pollution law, the Public Health Service Act of 1912, assigned Federal water quality responsibility to the Public Health Service.[6] The agency's antipollution mandate was limited to the study and investigation of the relationship between water pollution and the propagation of disease.

The waste-receptor/navigation trade-off was again the focus of concern in the Oil Pollution Act of 1924.[7] The Act prohibited vessels from dumping oil in navigable United States waters.

The 1948 Water Pollution Control Act   Concern with the broader trade-off between pollution and the full range of clean-water uses was not evident in Federal legislation until 1948. The 1948 Water Pollution Control Act specifically refers to benefits "to public health and *welfare*" (italics added) as the basis for the Federal role in water pollution control.[8] The 1948 Act provided the foundation upon which subsequent legislation has been built. Its main provisions were:

1. Administrative responsibility was vested in the Surgeon General of the Public Health Service. (The Public Health Service was, at that time, an agency of the Federal Security Administration.)
2. The prime regulatory provision of the Act made "subject to abatement" the pollution of "interstate waters" which "endangers the health or welfare of persons in a state other than that in which the discharge originates."
3. The abatement procedure specified by the Act involved the following steps:
    a. Determination by the Surgeon General that illegal pollution was taking place.
    b. Notification of the polluter and the pollution control agency (if any) of the originating state. Notification might include a recommendation of remedial measures and specification of "a reasonable time" for the offender to secure abatement.
    c. If the pollution was not abated, the Surgeon General would send a second notification to the above parties. The Surgeon General had the option of recommending that the state within which the pollution was originating initiate an abatement suit.
    d. In the event that pollution was still not abated and the originating state failed to file suit, the Federal Security Administrator would be authorized, within a "reasonable" time, to call a public hearing near the site of the discharge. The hearing board would then submit abatement recommendations to the Federal Security Administrator.
    e. Finally, if the board's recommendations were not implemented after the polluter had been afforded a "reasonable opportunity" to comply, the Administrator was authorized to request that the United States Attorney General bring suit to secure abatement. The Administrator could make this request only with the consent of the originating state.
    f. If pollution were proved, the courts were charged with ordering and enforcing abatement procedures "giving due consideration to the practicability and economic feasibility" of the abatement plan.
4. The prime fiscal element of the Act was the authorization of Federal loans to state and local governments for the construction of waste treatment facilities. Loans were limited to one-third of the project cost with a single-loan limit of $250,000.

The main provisions of the law indicate only a limited commitment to clean water. The Act, applying only to interstate waters, represented a step backwards from the 1899 law which had forbidden waste disposal in both interstate and intrastate waters. The Act did not forbid water pollution across-the-board. Abatement could be required only if the courts determined that pollution adversely affected health and welfare. The limited nature of the Federal commitment is also clear from the established enforcement mechanisms. First, the Act relied on state initiation of pollution abatement proceedings rather than direct Federal intervention. Abatement suits could only be brought at the request of the state in which the pollution originated. Given the unwillingness of a state government to risk imposing costs on owners and workers of polluting firms, reliance on state initiative seriously weakened the effectiveness of pollution-control enforcement. Second, the Act's enforcement mechanisms placed heavy emphasis on voluntary compliance with negotiated standards. Court action to require abatement could be used only as a last resort after an indefinite period of time. Third, each step required explicit exercise of administrative discretion. Appointed officials determined whether the process should be begun, accelerated, or brought to completion. Some analysts consider a decision-making process that relies heavily on administrative discretion an appropriate method of aggregating preferences. The process would permit the administrator ample opportunity to determine the force of conflicting interests and to devise a workable compromise. On the other hand, in terms of economically efficient decision-making, pecuniary interests should be ignored. In practice, pecuniary interests are not ignored, and the polluter may have considerable political influence on the administrator. Furthermore, the Act did not represent a decision about the trade-off between waste-receptor and clean-water use. In effect, it simply established a mechanism which would permit trade-off policy decisions to be made case-by-case in accordance with the relative intensity of support or opposition from affected parties.

Antipollution Legislation in the Fifties and Early Sixties   The 1948 Act, although originally due to expire in 1953, was extended, essentially unaltered, through 1956. The first substantive change in Federal pollution-control policy came in 1956.[9] The 1956 amendments shifted Federal construction aid from a loan to a grant basis. (No money had ever been appropriated under the 1948 Act's loan provisions.[10]) Limitations on Federal contributions of matching funds were set at thirty percent of project cost or $250,000 maximum.

The 1956 legislation extended the 1948 Act and added an informal conference prior to the public hearing. The law also permitted court action with the consent of either state involved in interstate pollution.

The basic outlines of Federal policy then remained stable until

1965. The intervening years can be divided into two periods. First, during the Eisenhower years, there was a struggle between advocates of increased Federal efforts and those, including the President, arguing for total reliance on state initiative. Second, during the early sixties, tentative efforts were made toward tangible program revisions.

The first stage culminated with a 1960 Presidential veto of a bill which would have nearly doubled authorizations for matching grant funds and would have extended the program through 1970. The veto was sustained in Congress, but the Administration's efforts had been at least partially stymied.[11] In both 1958 and 1959 Eisenhower's budget messages had included a request for the total elimination of the matching grants program, but the program continued on the basis of 1956 authorization levels. The conflict between the Eisenhower Administration and Congress manifested itself in declining requests and rising appropriations in the later years of the Administration.

In 1961, the new administration provided executive branch support for stronger legislation. Congress approved construction grant authorizations designed to double the 1960 level by 1967.[12] While the 30 percent of project cost limitation was retained, the maximum Federal contribution was raised to $600,000. The 1961 legislation also extended Federal abatement authority to all interstate and navigable waters, with the stipulation that the Secretary of Health, Education, and Welfare obtain the consent of the state governor before requesting that the Attorney General file suit against a polluter of intrastate waters.

Attempts to further revise the Federal program were continued into the early sixties with little success. In 1963 and 1964 the House failed to act on a Senate bill which would have expanded matching grant authorizations and maximum limits on Federal contributions to specific projects. The bill would have permitted the Secretary of Health, Education, and Welfare to set standards of water quality for interstate bodies of water when standards had not been established by a state.

The Water Quality Act of 1965   Senate and House hearings on the 1965 legislation revealed continuing industry opposition to an increased Federal role in pollution control. Industry representatives argued that water quality decisions should be made on a stream-by-stream basis and that states should have primary responsibility for pollution control. The Water Quality Act of 1965 emerged as an apparent victory for pollution control advocates.[13]

The 1965 legislation brought about several alterations in Federal antipollution law: [14]

1. The Act created a Water Pollution Control Administration (FWPCA) within the Department of Health, Education, and Welfare to administer the Federal water pollution program.
2. The central regulatory provision of the Act required that states establish water quality standards for interstate waters within their boundaries and develop plans for the implementation of those standards. Both standards and implementation plans were to be subject to the approval of the FWPCA.
3. The Act increased sewage treatment construction grant authorizations from $100 million to $150 million per year.
4. The Act permitted the Federal government to bypass the conference and public hearing procedures required by earlier legislation prior to filing an abatement suit, provided that the polluter was given 180 days advance notice.

In retrospect, what appeared to be a major step in the direction of improved enforcement may have been a Pyrrhic victory. Both proponents and opponents of an expanded Federal effort seemed to attach a great deal of significance to the possibility of replacing case-by-case enforcement with uniform, predetermined water quality standards. Sponsors argued that predetermined standards ". . . would make it possible to determine comparatively easily whether a discharge would cause (or was causing) pollution . . ." [15] In retrospect, the change to water quality standards may have weakened pollution abatement efforts. Under the pre-1965 legislation, the standard of water quality for a given stream would have been determined after the initiation of abatement proceedings. The determination would have been made either through the interaction of Health, Education, and Welfare representatives, state and local officials, and polluters at the conference stage, or by the courts. There is no reason to believe that court determinations of acceptable levels of pollution under the old act would have been either more or less strict than the new water quality standards.

Ultimate decisions about standards were still left to the courts by the 1965 Act. The courts were charged by the Act to give ". . . due consideration to the practicability and to the physical and economic feasibility of complying with such standards." [16] If a firm could argue successfully that pollution abatement would impose unbearable costs, the courts could permit the firm to continue functioning even though its effluents violated legislated standards.

The locus of enforcement power was rather circumscribed under the 1965 law. The Federal government could initiate abatement proceedings unilaterally only in instances of interstate pollution. In cases of intrastate pollution, Federal intervention could come about only at the request of the state.

The abatement process continued to emphasize voluntary compliance. Court action could be taken only after a conference and public hearing, except under the 180-day provision for Federal standards enforcement. The prime deficiencies (from the point of view of those wishing to accelerate cleanup) of the pre-1965 legislation lay in its enforcement procedures, which relied totally on administrative discretion. These enforcement mechanisms were retained in the 1965 law. Administrative discretion still dominated decisions to enforce standards.

The enforcement of standards also posed some legal difficulties. When more than one firm is discharging into a body of water, it is difficult to assign any one firm the legal blame for below standard water quality. As a result of this difficulty, the enforcement of stream standards became a process of state assignment of effluent limitations to specific firms through implementation plans subject to Federal approval. Uncertainty about the legal force of effluent standards was dispelled by the Federal government's response to the resurrection of the old Refuse Act.

The Refuse Act of 1899 Revisited The waste-disposal section of the 1899 Rivers and Harbors Act was rediscovered by environmentalists in 1970. The Nixon Administration moved immediately to incorporate the powers granted by the Act into the existing policy scheme. United States Attorneys were instructed not to prosecute polluters under the Act without clearance from the Justice Department in Washington, except in cases of "accidental or infrequent pollution." [17] This requirement was later removed as the Administration tied the Refuse Act's provisions to more recent law by establishing a national permit system requiring waste dischargers to apply for a permit by July, 1971. Permits were granted as long as already established state or Federal water quality standards would not be violated.[18]

The availability of Refuse Act provisions amounted to a considerable broadening of Federal powers. The enforcement provisions were much less restrictive than those of the 1965 Act in that (a) jurisdiction extended over all navigable waters, (b) criminal penalties (a $2500 fine or 6 months imprisonment), as well as injunctive relief, were provided, and (c) the conference-hearing procedure was not required.

Even though the permit system could be interpreted as undermining the potential pollution abatement authority granted the Federal government under the Refuse Act, its implementation improved on the 1965 Act in at least two respects. First, permit applications were expected to provide a wealth of previously unavailable information on sources of water pollution, and, second, the permit system provided a legal means for enforcing the effluent limitations assigned to implement stream standards. The emerging effluent control orientation of the Federal program was to be given a stronger legal foundation under the 1972 Water Pollution Control Act amendments.

Air Pollution Control

The Air Pollution Control Act of 1955 was the first major Federal legislation dealing with air quality. The Act authorized expenditures by the Surgeon General's office for research, training, and demonstration projects. In 1959, the $5 million authorization under the Act was extended to 1964. Senate efforts to expand Federal authority were abortive until the first permanent Federal air pollution legislation was passed in 1963.[19]

The 1963 Clean Air Act   The tone of the 1963 Clean Air Act reflected the unwillingness of some legislators to grant power to the Federal government at the expense of states and municipalities. However, limited enforcement authority was assumed by the Federal government. In cases of interstate pollution the Secretary of Health, Education, and Welfare was authorized to undertake abatement procedures roughly the same as the conference-hearing procedures provided in the water pollution control process. In cases of intrastate pollution, enforcement could be initiated at the request of state and local authorities. Ultimately, court action could lead to a cease and desist order. The Act also authorized expenditures to investigate technological progress to control auto emissions. In addition, the Act authorized matching grants to state and local agencies for up to two-thirds of the cost of developing air pollution control programs.

Auto Exhaust Pollution   Continuing concern with auto exhaust pollution led the Congress to pass the 1965 Motor Vehicle Air Pollution Control Act. The Act directed the Health, Education, and Welfare Secretary to set hydrocarbon and carbon monoxide emission standards for new motor vehicles giving consideration both to "health and welfare" and to technological feasibility and cost. The Act forbade the sale of new vehicles not meeting the standards. The Federal grant program initiated in 1963 was expanded in 1966 and again in 1967.

Air Quality Standards The 1967 Act constituted the first Federal step in the direction of air quality standards. Under the Act, the Secretary of Health, Education, and Welfare was authorized to designate air quality regions and to set and enforce air quality standards within such regions and in cases in which state, local, and regional authorities failed to act. Uniform national standards, although originally requested by the Johnson Administration, were purged from the final legislation. They had been the butt of strenuous opposition by industry representatives.[20] The standards approach to air pollution control has the same difficulties as the standards approach to water pollution control. It is exceedingly difficult to determine that any one firm is responsible for lowering air quality below the designated standard. The standards approach to air quality also opens up the possibility of actually reducing the quality of air in clean air regions. The marginal air polluter may cause a decrease in air quality, but not a sufficient decrease to result in a violation of the standard. The 1967 Act also permitted the Health, Education, and Welfare Secretary to seek court injunctions to curtail emissions when the public health was in "imminent and substantial" danger.

1970 Legislation Current air pollution control legislation reflects changes incorporated in the 1970 Environmental Quality Improvement Act. The most decisive step taken in the 1970 Act involved establishing, by Congressional action, automobile emission standards. The law stipulated that 1975 cars emit ninety percent less carbon monoxide and hydrocarbons than 1970 models and that 1976 models emit ninety percent less nitrogen oxides than 1971 models.[21] This action represented substantial change in two respects. First, it involved the first instance of emission standards for either air or water. Thus, the enforcement problems associated with receptor quality standards were avoided, at least in regard to auto emissions. Second, the Act also represented the first instance of a Federally *legislated* standard for either air or water. In previous Federal air pollution legislation, the Federal control over standards was in the hands of administrators.

The erosion of administrative discretion was further accelerated by a provision permitting citizen suits against administrators or violators (including governments). This provision should accelerate enforcement action. Finally, the Act provided fines and criminal penalties for persons violating implementation plans if prior requests for corrective action were not honored.

The Proposed Tax on Lead in Gasoline Lead added to gasoline to increase octane presents two problems. Its emission poses a potential health hazard and its presence in gas prevents the use of the catalytic emission control systems scheduled to be installed in cars by 1976 to control other types of auto emissions.

In his environmental message of February 8, 1971, President Nixon proposed a tax on lead in gasoline as a supplement to regulatory controls. In simple terms, the tax would be set at a level sufficient to give unleaded gasoline a price advantage in the market place. Without the tax on leaded gasoline, the higher production costs of unleaded gasoline would place unleaded gasoline at a price disadvantage. Imposing a tax sufficient to make unleaded gas relatively less expensive creates an economic incentive for private actions leading to lower levels of lead emissions. In effect, the proposed tax would be an economic lever to make pollution abatement activity economically rewarding to the individual. This proposal would require a minimum amount of administration and greatly reduce the enforcement problems and costs associated with the regulatory approach.

In spite of the intrinsic appeal of the tax approach, the proposal was discarded by the Nixon Administration and replaced by direct regulation of the lead content of automotive gasoline.[22] In February, 1972, the Environmental Protection Agency announced a set of rules designed to insure the availability of one grade of lead-free and phosphorus-free gasoline by July 1, 1974, and a phased reduction of the lead content of "regular" and "premium" gasolines beginning January 1, 1974, and culminating January 1, 1977. The goal is to reduce lead emissions from automobiles by 60 to 65 percent by mid-1977. As is always the case with direct regulation, there is a set of comprehensive rules designed to insure compliance with the goal. The proposed rules contain various provisions indicating which service stations are affected by the regulation, the manner by which wholesale and retail distributors are to prove that they have complied with the rules, and specific rules on the size of nozzles and filler pipes required to insure that the cheaper leaded gasoline will not be pumped into cars designed to run on lead-free gasoline.

The Sulfur Tax In addition to proposing a tax on leaded gasoline, President Nixon has also proposed that a tax be levied on emissions of sulfur dioxides. Over a year elapsed between the announcement and the appearance of the actual proposal. One of the key aspects of the plan is that the tax would not apply in those areas in which the general air quality is already above Federal standards. Critics of the plan immediately responded to this provision.[23] They argue that the proposal would allow relatively clean areas of the country to become more polluted in the process of reducing pollution levels in the less clean areas. Applying the tax in dirty areas and exempting clean areas certainly creates an economic incentive for industries producing significant amounts of sulfur dioxides to escape the tax by moving to relatively clean areas. The economic incentive for moves could be eliminated simply by making the tax applicable to all areas.

Why was such a stipulation incorporated into the proposal? Congressional investigations have been made into the charge that political factors were responsible for the regional aspects of the sulfur tax proposal. The copper industry produces significant amounts of sulfur dioxide but would generally escape the tax because thirteen of its fifteen smelters are located in Western states where overall state air quality levels exceed the Federal requirement in spite of low quality levels in those areas adjacent to copper smelters. The Senate Air and Water Pollution Subcommittee has investigated charges that the White House attempted to force the state of Montana to lower its air pollution standards.[24] The reduction would benefit the copper industry because the proposed Montana air quality standards would require higher air quality than would be necessitated by Federal standards. At the hearings, EPA Administrator William D. Ruckelshaus denied the allegation that his agency's ultimate decision not to support Montana's standards for sulfur dioxide emissions from copper smelters was a decision dictated by the White House.[25]

The events surrounding the proposed tax on sulfur dioxide indicate that even the relatively small amounts of regulation required in pollution control systems based on a tax or charge system make formulating a general environmental program an intensely political process.

The Effectiveness of Policies

In spite of the number of laws passed prior to 1972 to deal with air and water pollution, some basic problems remained unsolved. The three issues mentioned at the start of this chapter are considered in this section.

Assignment of the Policy-Making Task   Responsibility for administering Federal environmental legislation rests primarily on the Environmental Protection Agency. The EPA was created in 1970 as a distinct Federal agency combining within its mandate the main provisions of the Water Pollution Control Act and the Clean Air Act. The agency encompasses earlier administrative units which had previously been lodged elsewhere in the bureaucracy and is responsible directly to the President.

Broader staff functions are performed by the Council on Environmental Quality. The three-man council is patterned after the Council of Economic Advisors and is responsible for preparing an annual report making recommendations to the President. Efforts to follow the Employment Act model by establishing a Joint Congressional Committee on the Environment have not come to fruition.

Are these policy-making arrangements appropriate for the task at hand? Until the Federal government exerted its first legislative influence on the choice of alternative uses for air and water, use decisions were made on the basis of what might be called a "common law" model. Legal tradition had assigned water use rights to riparian owners, and the general public had no legal standing to contest the "reasonableness" of water uses. A plaintiff seeking pollution abatement had to show damage to his property in order for his case to be heard by the courts. Public nuisance charges could be made only by the state, and pollution was not included in the concept of public nuisance. The general public had no real say in the use of water. Those decisions now considered to be societal decisions were made through separate adjudications of private disputes.

Leaving aside the Refuse Act of 1899, the exercise of policy-making power was avoided by the Federal legislature and was assigned to state legislatures or administrators if they wished to use their powers. Standard-setting in the water quality area is still basically a state function with administrative backup at the Federal level. Air quality standard-setting is largely a Federal function, with heavy reliance on EPA support to the states in formulating implementation plans.

The continuing evolution of the decision-making mechanism seems to be replacing administrative determination of standards with legislatively established standards to be enforced by the administrators. The legislative determination of auto emission control standards and the 1972 Water Pollution Control Act are evidence of the more active role of the Congress in the standards determination process.

Assignment of the policy-making role is difficult because there are few a priori reasons to expect one group of policy-makers to make better social decisions than any other group. There is no political model analogous to the economist's predictive models to forecast the outcome of policy decisions by various groups. Therefore, the selection of a policy-making body must be based on the attempt to eliminate possible biases in the decision-making process. For example, experience has indicated that the competition between states for new industry tends to make the states less than perfect enforcers of environmental standards. Also, the preferences of polluters for state regulation and the preference of environmentalists for Federally legislated standards indicates that both camps assume that Federal standards will be more effective.

There is no a priori way to determine whether legislated standards will be more effective than standards determined by administrative agencies. Both the administrators and the legislators will be subject to pressure from the polluters and the environmentalists; and in both cases the influence of special interest groups fearing monetary losses is likely to outweigh the influence of those citizens who have no direct monetary concern with decisions made.

The Development of Standards for Performance   The development of standards for environmental quality is at best an inexact art. It is possible to argue that a firm set of standards cannot be developed until the public is able to assess the costs and benefits of various degrees of environmental improvement. This line of reasoning would suggest that standards would be changed frequently as better cost-benefit information becomes available.

The development of standards for water quality has not been a very satisfactory process from the point of view of the environmentalist. The 1965 Act required adoption of standards and implementation plans by June 30, 1967. By June 30, 1969, standards for all states had been approved by the Federal government. In August, 1970, the implementation plans of some states had still not been approved.[26] Thus, difficulties arose right at the start of the process. Similar delays have plagued the process of Federal approval of state implementation plans under the Clean Air Act.

One way of explaining this lag in the process is to examine the political restraints facing the Federal administrators. The Federal government requires the political backing of the states if water quality is to be improved.[27] Yet the states are independent political entities. If a state feels threatened by Federal standards which might interfere with its economic development plans, the state can, through its Congressmen, exert influence on the agency or on the Executive. The fact that as of April, 1969, thirty states had yet to include an anti-degradation clause in their standards illustrates the power of the states to resist Federal guidelines.[28] Thus, it is not surprising that Federal administrators will attempt to compromise and bargain on state standards.

A second explanation of the slowness with which standards have been developed places more of the blame on the Federal administrators. The Nader task force's examination of the Federal role in setting water quality standards is particularly critical. Although the Water Quality Act and the Federal Water Pollution Control Administration's Guidelines call for standards designed to "enhance the quality of water," the task force has argued that the "standards FWQA [FWPCA] was actually approving showed the Guideline had no meaning in practice." The task force cites the Illinois standards which had been approved by the Federal government in 1968:

Lake Michigan's actual measured level of dissolved solids is about 155 milligrams per liter (mg/l). The Illinois standard permits the annual average of dissolved solids to go to 165 mg/l — 10 mg/l higher than it is already in this polluted lake. The present level of cyanide in the lake is about 0.01 mg/l; the Illinois standard is 2½ times as high, 0.025 mg/l. In some Illinois streams there is presently no oil to be found. Yet the standards say only that oil shall not be permitted in such amounts as will create a fire hazard, coat boat hulls or injure fish, thus implying that at least some oil is acceptable where none existed before.[29]

While the Nader report implies (without citing further instances) that reduction in water quality was commonly permitted in Federally approved state standards, the report does not indicate the frequency with which standards would, if enforced, bring about improvements in water quality. The Nader presentation also illustrates the difficulty of attaching value to measures of pollution. Does a 10 mg/1 increase in dissolved solids have any effect on water values? The extent to which degradation would be permitted under approved standards is difficult to determine. Although states were required by Federal guidelines to promise not to permit lower water quality in drawing up standards and implementation plans, the FWPCA did not require states to submit a description of the current condition of the waters.[30]

Progress Toward the Goal? The evidence on the degree of progress toward cleaner air and water as a result of the Federal legislation is limited by the difficulty of measurement. For example, how polluted would the nation's air and water be if these laws had never been passed? Or how much additional quality improvement would there have been if the enforcement had been more strict? Lack of evidence is also attributable to the absence of ongoing monitoring of pollution levels.

Two studies do provide some evidence on the progress to date. First, the Environmental Protection Agency has estimated that the total biological oxygen demand (BOD) of wastes discharged into United States water in 1968 was "only slightly" larger than in 1957. This relative constancy of organic waste discharges over the period was maintained in the face of a doubling in the total BOD production.[31] Although the United States might have been holding the line on organic waste discharges, the Council on Environmental Quality reported that "the overall quality of the Nation's waters probably has deteriorated because of accelerated eutrophication [that is, aging of water bodies because of the growth of plants], increased discharges of toxic materials, greater bodies of sediment, and other factors." [32]

Physical measures of pollution do not indicate the true relative social costs of each type of discharge. In general, threats to public health have been weighed more heavily than recreational or esthetic considerations. Thus, the crackdown on mercury discharges during 1970 and 1971 was swift and apparently decisive. The Refuse Act of 1899 provided the legal basis for actions against mercury pollution. Although technically the Act's provisions permit quick responses to other kinds of pollutants, apparently the bureaucracy has arrived at the judgment that less immediately harmful discharges may as well be handled in the context of stream standards and through the negotiation process.

The CEQ has also reported measurements of short-run changes in air quality. In general, air pollution, measured by weight of various kinds of pollutants, is increasing nationwide — an increase of 3.2 percent between 1968 and 1969. Each type of pollutant, with the exception of transportation and solid waste disposal, showed an increase. The decline in solid waste disposal, the CEQ speculates, reflected a decrease in open burning in municipal dumps. The decline in transportation emissions, again according to the CEQ, reflected the replacement of older vehicles by newer vehicles with emission control devices. [33]

Only one aspect of the Federal pollution abatement program has been subjected to a detailed evaluation. The General Accounting Office (GAO) conducted a study of the Federal waste treatment facility construction program and found that in the eight states examined the construction program had not yielded an increase in water quality. [34] Although individual waste treatment facilities in many cases improved the quality of municipal effluents, the increase in pollution from industrial sources was more than enough to offset gains. The GAO's findings highlighted the lack of coordination between the construction grants program and the state plans for curbing industrial and other sources of pollution. Specifically, the GAO concluded that grants were distributed on a "first come–first served" basis and not in relation to expected benefits. [35] As a result, Federal and local capital expenditures and local operating costs had been incurred with no substantial impact on water quality.

The GAO study also noted the frequent use of municipal facilities to treat industrial wastes. The CEQ has recently reported that for the nation as a whole, "50 percent of the wastes treated in municipal plants are from industrial sources. . . ."[36]

The GAO's conclusions with respect to poor planning and lack of coordination between the granting agency (FWPCA) and the grant recipient were documented in several case studies. In one instance, treatment facilities financed in part by the grant program were found to be discharging waste into a stream for extended periods of near-zero flow. The report cites the reply of an FWPCA official to inquiries as to how the decision was made to fund these projects:

. . . the three projects were approved as being included in a list of municipalities in need of waste treatment facilities, which was published in the Federal Register. Such lists . . . merely identified municipalities in need of sewerage facilities in the State, in alphabetical order, and did not indicate the priority of projects.[37]

In a rare bit of bureaucratic sarcasm, the report notes that a new comprehensive plan drawn up for the area in which the plants were functioning called for their abandonment and replacement:

In this regard, the plan described the tributary as "grossly polluted" and *attributed this condition primarily to the large number of treatment plants discharging their effluent into the tributary.*[38] (Italics added.)

The study group also determined that the level of appropriations of Federal funds was inadequate to the implementation plans of the states. In one state which had planned a nine-year construction program it was estimated by GAO that the current (1969) levels of funding of grants to the state would permit completion of the program in thirty years! [39]

The limited progress made to date has involved considerable cost. At the time of the GAO study the Federal government had awarded approximately $1.2 billion in waste treatment grants. Combined with state and local shares, the total cost of municipal treatment facilities through 1969 amounted to about $5.4 billion. In its 1971 report, the CEQ estimated the replacement value of existing municipal waste treatment plants at over $6 billion in 1970. An additional replacement cost of $7.6 billion for "interception sewers, pumping stations, and outfalls associated with the waste treatment plants" yields a total of $13.7 billion in existing capital for municipal treatment systems.[40]

The EPA has estimated figures for treatment of industrial wastes before discharge into water bodies. In 1970 waste treatment facilities in manufacturing were estimated to have a $3.9 billion replacement value.[41] Operating costs in 1970 were estimated at $1.2 billion for municipal waste treatment facilities and $0.8 billion for industrial waste treatment facilities.[42]

Cumulative investment to 1970 in air pollution control equipment was estimated by the EPA at $0.2 billion out of public funds (for Federal facilities only) and $1.1 billion by industry, with annual operating costs of $0.1 billion and $0.7 billion respectively.[43]

These costs are those associated, roughly, with achieving the levels of air and water quality which prevailed in 1970. Achievement of standards scheduled to be met by 1975 will require a doubling of annual costs (interest, depreciation of capital equipment, and operating expenditures) between 1970 and 1975. The total costs that must be incurred between 1970 and 1975 to meet air and water quality standards are estimated at $62 billion. This total excludes an estimated cost of between $15 billion and $48 billion for dealing with overflow problems resulting from the use of combined storm and sanitary sewers.[44]

While more studies of program performance are needed, the evidence to date indicates that progress has been slow and in spite of already high costs, more money will have to be spent, and spent sooner, if legislative goals are to be realized. In the area of water pollution control, some of the problems dealt with in this section may have provided a stimulus for program alterations adopted at the Federal level in 1972.

The Water Pollution Control Act Amendments of 1972. On October 18, 1972, the Federal Water Pollution Control Act Amendments became law over President Nixon's veto. The Act brought several major changes in Federal policy, some of which respond to those factors noted above as apparent weaknesses in the 1965 Act.

On the surface, the most striking provisions of the Act define national water quality goals: ". . . that the discharge of pollutants into the navigable waters be eliminated by 1985" and that ". . . an interim goal of water quality which provides for the protection and propagation of fish, shellfish, and wildlife and provides for recreation in and on the water be achieved by July 1, 1983."[45] While this statement of goals generated a good deal of publicity and a degree of controversy when the Act became law, it should be kept in mind that these goals merely constitute a statement of national purpose and do not have the force of legally established water quality standards. Whether the goals will be achieved depends on the effectiveness of specific programs designed and given legal force by the Act.

Movement in the direction of the stated goals is to be accomplished by the achievement of specific effluent standards. For privately owned point sources of pollution the Act mandates, by July 1, 1977, effluent limitations which ". . . shall require the application of the best practicable control technology currently available," and, by July 1, 1983, effluent limitations which ". . . shall require application of the best available technology economically achievable for such category or class, which will result in reasonable further progress toward the national goal. . . ." [46]

For publicly owned treatment works, the Act requires "secondary treatment" by 1977 and the "best practicable waste treatment technology" by 1983.[47] The key terms in this policy statement are to be defined by the EPA Administrator.

The Act's implementation mechanism is essentially that which had been evolving under the combined powers of the 1965 Act and the Refuse Act of 1899; that is, state established and Federally approved water quality standards and implementation plans would be retained. A Federal-state permit system based on existing implementation plans would allow exceptions to a zero discharge goal. Enforcement of effluent limitations is assigned initially to the states, with provisions instructing the EPA to intervene if, in the Administrator's judgment, states are failing to enforce permit restrictions. The Act "authorizes" the Administrator to initiate civil actions for the enforcement of abatement orders.[48] An allowance for citizen participation in the enforcement process is made in the form of citizens' suits against the EPA for failing to act when required to do so by the Act or against polluters violating effluent limitations.[49] The Act has several provisions which have the effect of encouraging the development of abatement planning covering entire river basins and it requires that user charges be levied on industrial users of publicly funded waste treatment works.

As has been the case historically with pollution control legislation, the Act offers as much of the appearance of change as of change itself. Administrative actions had already begun the implementation of a nationwide permit system. The 1972 legislation pulls together the threads of the already existing Federal program into one piece of legislation, which may have the effect of increasing the enforceability of the permit system.

The Act also appears to be distinctive in that it comes close to actual *legislative* determination of water pollution control policy. For public pollution sources — waste treatment works — this is clearly the case. The legislation requires secondary treatment at all sources by 1977. This requirement is analogous to the requirement for reduced auto emissions legislated in the Clean Air Act. To some extent, then, traditional reliance on administrative discretion or state action in standard-setting is eroded in favor of Federal legislative control. Yet, for nonpublic pollution sources this is by no means the case. Vagueness in the law's wording — "best practicable" and "best available" technology — still provides a broad range of administrative discretion in establishing effluent limitations. Presumably, of course, the EPA will feel constrained by the goals specified in the Act and by subsequent actions of the Congress in reviewing progress under the Act. But even the secondary treatment requirement may be expected to be weakened when it comes to the enforcement stage. The EPA may be expected to be somewhat reluctant to bring suit against states and municipalities without extensive prior efforts to achieve voluntary compliance. Furthermore, it should be kept in mind that the Act does not require the Adminstrator to bring court action; it merely authorizes him to do so. Voluntarism is thus retained at the crucial enforcement stage.

While movement away from administrative discretion may seem, and in certain respects is, desirable, it has its costs. The effluent limitation approach, as it is being implemented for municipal sources and as it is likely to be implemented for industrial sources through performance standards, specifies uniform levels of treatment at all point sources. The requirement of uniform treatment may be exceedingly costly from some points of view. If we accept current, legally mandated water quality standards as goals, there is little doubt that such standards can be achieved at lower cost than those which will be incurred with uniform treatment. In general, it is unlikely that all sources of pollution in a river system will make the same contribution to decreases in water quality. Differences in a river's hydrological characteristics from stretch to stretch — primarily differences in rates of flow or volume of water — mean that a given amount of effluent may reduce the stream below standard at some points and not reduce it below standard at others. Hence, requiring the same level of treatment at all sources may simply constitute a waste of funds. Any saving that might be obtained by a least-cost assignment of treatment responsibility will be lost by uniform treatment requirements. In this regard, the Act is rather contradictory. Least-cost abatement schemes are probably best designed and implemented on a basin-wide level. Although it seems to encourage the development of basin-wide planning, the Act forecloses at the same time those options which would make basin-wide planning desirable.

On the most general level, the Act has been attacked on the grounds that the zero pollution goal is economically inefficient and that the marginal cost of the last units of abatement is likely to be both extremely high and far in excess of marginal benefits at near-zero discharge. Most economists would probably agree with this contention, but the criticism of the Act implicit in the contention is not valid. The specific provisions of the Act clearly suggest that there is a greater likelihood of underachievement than of overachievement of the stated goals.

10

Nonmarket Solutions to Environmental Problems

As the previous chapter indicated, most past environmental action has been based upon direct governmental regulation of pollution. Direct regulation is a nonmarket approach to the problem. This chapter considers nonmarket solutions to the environmental problem. The economist usually has a built-in bias, of which the reader should be aware, in favor of market systems for the allocation of resources. The market oriented systems are considered in the following chapter.

One nonmarket process for environmental action might be termed "ecotage" (an analogy with the word *sabotage*). This type of individual or group action, characterized by dramatic gestures such as dumping sewage outflows on rugs in the offices of executives of polluting firms, may be effective but it is illegal. Thus, the methodology of "The Fox" — the legendary ecotage expert of the Chicago area — cannot be considered as a general scheme for long-run environmental action.

Among the more rational methods of nonmarket control are environmental action through the legal system and general regulatory approaches to environmental policy.

Legal Remedies and Environmental Control

Ultimately, the court system will play a critical role in the selection of an environmental policy because of its ability to question the constitutionality of legislation, interpret complex and often vague legislation, and review the controversial actions of administrative agencies. This role of the court is not our present concern. The immediate goal is to examine the capabilities of the legal process to be the vehicle for environmental change.

One environmental law expert, Joseph L. Sax, has proposed a more active role for the courts in conjunction with the legislative function of policy determination.[1] Sax suggests activation of the legal notion of the state as a trustee of common property resources. The concept has not often been used in the United States, but in some instances the courts have been willing to attempt to strike a balance "which is designed to retain the largest measure of public use consistent with needful development and industrialization." [2] Sax cites cases in which the courts have thrust back upon legislatures the responsibility for making specific decisions on trade-offs between environmental and esthetic values on the one hand and industrial development on the other.[3] Each case served to focus political concern on the general issues of environmental policy-making. While the public trust notion has received little attention as the basis for litigation, each case which forces the legislature to review administrative discretion reinforces the policy-making power of legislatures relative to the bureaucracy.

Greater application of the public trust notion would make possible more private suits against polluters and destroy the notion that only riparian rights will be adjudicated by the courts. Giving the public the right to sue on esthetic grounds would open a whole new approach to environmental improvement.

Attractive as the idea of suing the polluters appears to be, however, the judicial approach may have fairly limited possibilities as a *general* environmental control system. Since courts rule on *specific* cases and not on general principles, each polluter of air or water might have to be the subject of a separate suit. The courts could be jammed up for years to come. Furthermore, the concept of complete judicial determination of the use of air and water does not place decision-making responsibility in the proper place. The elected representatives of the public should make policy — not the courts system. It is one thing to ask the courts to review the reasonableness of administrative policy or to force the legislature to take action but they cannot be asked to be primary policy-makers. Finally, while environmental action groups have funds to take a few major cases to court, they cannot finance suits against all polluters. Private suits by local action groups against local polluters present the problems of sharing costs and the "free rider" discussed in Chapter 8.

It is unlikely, then, that the legal approach can be the major vehicle for environmental improvement. The courts will decide many environmental questions in the course of time, but the role of the judiciary must remain the traditional one of evaluating the constitutionality of legislative action, reviewing administrative decisions, and resolving specific cases of law. The judiciary cannot be asked to resolve all the "hard" issues of public policy; the legislative branch of government must take on that responsibility.

The Regulatory Approach to Environmental Policy

Most current environmental action relies upon the use of regulatory mechanisms. Congress has seen fit, except in a few recent instances, to develop basic principles and rely upon a Federal bureaucracy to refine and apply these principles and guidelines.

The use of regulation is by no means new or unique to the environmental case. The Federal Communications Commission, the Securities and Exchange Commission, the Food and Drug Administration, the Interstate Commerce Commission, and the Civil Aeronautics Board are only a few of the better known Federal regulatory agencies. Having relied on the regulatory approach for many years, we are in a position to evaluate regulation in general as well as the regulatory approach to environmental improvement.

The Concept of Regulation   Direct regulation of business activity by government has become an increasingly important aspect of the United States economy. The emergence and growth of independent regulatory commissions represents an attempt to respond to specific problems. Initially, Congress attempted to handle the task of regulating business activity, but, given the size and complexity of the task, it was soon clear that Congress would not be able to discharge these responsibilities. Consequently, Congress created various independent regulatory agencies and assigned specific responsibilities to each agency.

Federal regulatory commissions have several common features. A commission is usually composed of five to seven individual commissioners appointed by the President with the consent of the Senate. The law usually requires that both major political parties be represented on a commission. Appointees generally serve long and overlapping terms; once appointed, individual commissioners are protected from dismissal except for malfeasance. In a further attempt to insure independence in decision-making, actions by regulatory commissions are subject to judicial reversal but usually are not subject to veto by the legislature or the executive branch of government.

Historically, regulation by independent commissions has been justified on several grounds. First, it is often argued that only specialized and independent regulatory bodies are capable of developing the special expertise necessary to deal with complex and technical regulatory problems. Independent commissions are viewed as better able than Congress to attract the technical and scientific staff necessary to formulate policy in a modern, technological society. Second, it is argued that commissions, being independent, are isolated from political influence by the executive and legislative branches. This freedom should allow commissions to devote themselves to protecting the public interest. Third, independence is claimed to isolate the regulatory commission and commissioners from control by the regulated industries. Fourth, because of the technical expertise of individual commissions, it is felt that decision-making through regulatory agencies will be less formal and more flexible than judicial decision-making. These arguments in favor of the regulatory approach do not exhaust all justifications but they are sufficiently comprehensive to indicate the public reasons commonly offered in support of regulatory commissions.[4]

Students of regulatory matters have engaged in endless debates about the validity of the a priori arguments advanced in favor of a regulatory approach. The "expertise" argument is questioned on the grounds that if a commissioner is an expert in a highly technical area, this expertise, rather than being an asset, is likely to be a liability in terms of policy-making ability. To be effective policy-makers, commissioners must be able to evaluate policy options from many perspectives, including, but not limited to the technological, economic, and social settings. With such requirements, the commissioner-technician can easily find himself unqualified and unable to act. The result could be a rigid and myopic public policy. This argument, of course, does not totally discredit the regulatory approach because regulatory agencies can develop expertise at the staff level. However, at the same time, there is no reason to suppose that regulatory commissions have any greater ability to attract experts than do the legislative or executive branches. Thus, the expertise argument in support of the regulatory approach is substantially weakened.

A stronger argument in favor of regulatory commissions is the belief that they will operate independently of Congress and the executive branch of government and, as a result, be unwavering in their devotion to the public interest. In any case, independence is a relative term, and regulation, regardless of the degree of independence, is going to be an intensely political process, because the policy decisions have a critical impact on the value of property rights of affected parties. There is no way to keep politics out of regulatory decision-making.

The above discussion should indicate that there is substantial disagreement on the validity of the a priori justifications for the regulatory approach. These disagreements tend to weaken the arguments of the supporters of the regulatory approach to economic problems.

The Ash Report   The scope of this book does not allow a complete review of the regulatory experience in the United States. There have been numerous Presidential Commissions charged with studying the problems of Federal regulatory commissions. Invariably they find that commissions overemphasize their judicial role at the expense of broad policy formulation. Regulators tend to be rigid and lack imagination in approaching new problems. Each study group recommends various changes, but there has been little improvement in regulatory performance. The most recent Presidential Commission, often referred to as the Ash Council in reference to its chairman Roy L. Ash of Litton Industries, described the present situation in the following terms:

The independent regulatory commissions, now mature institutions of the Federal government, are characterized by rigidity in their patterns of relationship with Congress and the executive branch, the regulated industries and the public. They lack the adaptive force which might regenerate or redefine their roles in helping shape the American economy.[5]

The study group also notes that the rigidity and lack of adaptability occurs at a time

. . . when persistent trends and new directions in the economy demand flexibility and imagination to carry out regulatory objectives and to formulate action in the interest of the public including the regulated segments of the private sector.[6]

According to the Ash Council, the major characteristics of present-day regulatory bodies are the collegial nature of agency organization, the judicial nature of agency activities, and the misalignment of functions among Federal agencies. The collegial nature of regulatory agencies arises from the fact that commissions usually consist of a number of coequal commissioners. This organizational structure, while designed to guard against arbitrary decisions and to insure that conflicting viewpoints will be considered, lacks clear lines of responsibility and leads to shared indecision and unaccountability. The Ash Report concludes that the collegial form promotes administrative inefficiency.

Congress originally intended that regulatory agencies would develop broad public policy in certain areas of the economy. Agencies have become too involved in quasi-judicial and judicial functions such as issuing complaints, litigating cases, and reviewing the decisions of hearing examiners. As a result, their entire operations are primarily shaped and determined by legal considerations at the expense of policy-making responsibilities.

The final defect noted by the Ash Report, a misalignment of functions, is well illustrated by the transportation sector. Regulatory responsibility is shared among the Interstate Commerce Commission (ICC), the Civil Aeronautics Board (CAB), and the Federal Maritime Commission (FMC). The ICC, established by Congress in 1887, is the oldest regulatory agency and has jurisdiction over railroads, trucks, busses, freight forwarders, barge lines, and pipelines. Regulation of airlines is conducted by the CAB, while the FMC controls maritime shipping. With different agencies having responsibilities in the transportation area, policy has become fragmented and rigid. In fact, most students of regulatory policy view transportation regulation as a prime example of regulatory failure. The inflexibility of policy has led to a situation in which "the economic absurdities cry out that some action should at long last be taken." [7]

Having noted defects in the regulatory process, the Ash Council, following in the steps of its predecessors, offers several recommendations for improvements. In most cases multi-member commissions should be replaced by a single administrator. The report predicts that this change would enhance the ability to attract highly qualified executives, place a greater reliance on informal rulemaking rather than on case-by-case adjudication, and permit a greater delegation of authority and staff accountability. In order to correct the undue emphasis on judicial action, there should be a drastic change in the procedures for commission review of hearing examiner decisions. Under the single administrative setup, reviews would be on a selective basis. Under the present procedure nearly all decisions can be, and usually are, reviewed by the regulatory commission. This change is intended to reduce the legal tone and character of an agency's operations. In addition, judicial review of agency decisions would be undertaken by a new Administrative Court of the United States capable of handling substantive issues in the areas of transportation, securities, and power legislation. Removing review from common law courts would, in the opinion of the Ash Report, reduce agency preoccupation with judicial form and procedures. These recommendations are intended to correct a situation in which

the present Commissions combine the passive, judicial characteristics of a court with the active policy responsibilities of an administrator, to the detriment of both.[8]

There is little to indicate, however, that the proposed changes would represent substantial improvements. The Ash Report suggests that a principal cause of regulatory failure is the organization of regulation, but reorganization alone is probably not sufficient to improve regulatory performance. Critics of the Ash Report point out that organizational changes do not alter the environment in which regulatory decision-making is conducted.[9] Basic changes, according to the experts, are required in the legal, political, and procedural setting, the expertise of the decision-makers, and the legislative mandate.[10] Simple reorganization is not likely to cause such changes.

Further Problems with Regulation   Because regulation is a nonmarket process for the allocation of resources, economists do not have a model to explain its workings. Assumptions about the economic effects of regulation substitute for a formal model. The commonly held view of regulation is described by Lee Loevinger, a former member of the Federal Communications Commission:

There seems to be an assumption that regulation acts simply and directly and that the issuance of a rule or an order by an administrative agency results in the achievement of the mandate and the purpose of that rule or order without any complicating consequences. This assumption is not to be found explicitly in any discussion but seems to be implied in most of the literature. To say the least, this assumption is uncritical, naive, and unrealistic.[11]

In contrast with the competitive model, regulatory decision-making involves a greater element of personal subjectivity. The motivations and incentives of participants are never fully known, and as a result, it is impossible to predict the workings of regulatory agencies. The danger is that the subjective elements inherent in the nature of the regulatory process could become a basis for decision-making.

Loevinger indicates that, historically, maximization of an agency's power has been the guiding principle behind regulatory decisions.[12] He bases his contention on the observation that there are few examples of regulatory bodies seeking a diminution of their power and responsibilities, but there are many examples of agency attempts to expand their powers. While the evidence is consistent with his hypothesis, any conclusions must remain tentative.

A fourth feature of regulation is its tendency to be self-expanding.[13] This tendency, while consistent with the power hypothesis, may simply be a reflection of the fact that an economy is composed of interrelated parts. As a result, public policy affecting one small part may easily produce effects in other unregulated areas and create a rationale or need for an expansion of regulation. Perhaps the best example of the self-expanding nature of regulation is the oil industry.[14] Initially, depletion allowances were adopted to increase oil production by providing additional economic incentives. Output increased and oil prices fell. Various production control schemes were then instituted to protect prices. The increased flow of domestic oil and falling crude prices led to the adoption of restrictions on the importation of foreign oil. The result is an oil industry which, through public policy, has been transformed into a cartel.

Finally, regulation tends to maintain the status quo. Some students of regulation have attributed this tendency to the fact that, in government, top managers who are responsible for innovations and changes tend to adopt a short-run view. The top positions in government are usually political appointments and the turnover rate is high. Each occupant of the office neglects the long-run, and the short-run perspective is not conducive to developing dynamic policies.[15] The status quo is also preserved by agency policy with respect to new entry into a regulated industry. The entry of new firms is discouraged because it may have a negative impact on existing firms. Thus, maintenance of the status quo creates an entry barrier to new firms and confers benefits to the established firms.

All of the points which have been made relative to the problems of regulation should make us skeptical of the wisdom of applying the general regulatory approach to the environmental improvement problem.

Is the Pollution Problem Different?   The regulatory approach to economic problems has been a general failure in the United States. Before this approach to environmental problems can be rejected, however, it is necessary to question whether pollution problems are sufficiently unique that success could be expected from the regulation of pollution. Is there any reason to be optimistic, to believe that the regulatory approach, in spite of its past failures, can be successfully applied in the environmental area?

Several aspects of pollution control suggest a negative answer. An understanding of pollution requires a highly technical and scientific base. The formulation of the proper policy must rest upon scientific knowledge. It is therefore likely that regulatory bodies will become saturated with the technical and scientific aspects of pollution control and, as has happened in the past, the agency will tend to become rigid and unable to formulate broad policies. In addition, the technical nature of pollution abatement suggests that the general public will be unable and unwilling to maintain their interest in it. Once the public loses interest in a regulatory body's actions, the regulatory agency tends to identify with the interests of the regulated firms. There is little reason to expect that the public interest for environmental improvement will be able to maintain its input into the regulatory decision-making process. The private interests are organized and can lobby for their position in a unified manner. The public interest, especially in the case of pollution control, is spread over many unorganized and fragmented individuals. Of course, certain environmental groups do offer a means of organizing the public, but these groups, compared to industry trade associations, are underfinanced, and their long-run viability is questionable. Thus, the unevenness with which private and public interests in environmental problems are organized suggests that, in the long run, the regulatory approach would favor private interests over public interests.

Moreover, an environmental improvement policy is certain to have negative economic effects in certain cases. Conflicts between a cleaner environment and powerful private economic interests cannot be avoided. Can the regulatory agency treat opposing economic interests in an equitable manner? Past history suggests that there is a strong likelihood that private economic interests will eventually gain substantial control of the regulatory process.

Finally, a regulatory approach would involve significant enforcement activities through the Federal courts. In the past, regulatory agencies presented with enforcement responsibilities have, according to the Ash Council, adopted a judicial and passive approach to their duties and, as a result, their broad policy making roles have been sacrificed. The likelihood of this happening with an environmental regulatory agency is obviously great. These features of the pollution problem bear a close resemblance to other economic problems which have been dealt with through the regulatory approach. In light of past events, regulation does not appear to be capable of the task.

There are two aspects of the pollution problem which offer some hope that regulation could be effective. First, the present great demand for a better environment is a strong positive force to which the regulatory body must respond. When public interest is at a high pitch, the regulatory approach has a chance for success. If public interest lessens, as is very likely, the possibility of success through regulation would diminish rapidly. Second, unlike public utility regulation, pollution regulation would require only partial control of the firm's activities. This reduces the resources necessary to conduct effective legislation. On balance, though, the disadvantages of control of the environment through a regulatory agency seem heavily to outweigh the advantages.

Current Regulation of the Environment   The EPA, headed by a Presidential appointee, is essentially a regulatory commission and is subject to all of the problems of regulatory agencies. The creation of the EPA, however, does not necessarily indicate that the United States has chosen direct regulation as the general means of managing the environment. Once environmental quality standards have been established, the EPA could rely on either direct regulation, a system of charges, or some combination of the two to insure that private use of the environment will be consistent with the established quality standards.

Certainly some direct regulation will be needed. In those cases where pollution creates an obvious health hazard or where the esthetic damage is overwhelming, direct regulation is the proper approach. But these cases cannot be used to argue that the entire environmental policy should be based on the regulatory approach.

The regulatory approach used thus far by the EPA has already started to reveal weaknesses which indicate that this attempt at regulation is not likely to be more successful than past regulatory efforts. The enforcement process, especially in the case of water pollution, has come to be a long, cumbersome, and costly process. The EPA shows signs of taking on the judicial atmosphere so common to regulatory bodies. Firms and municipalities have been able to delay, or even avoid, orders to change their discharge levels. The Council on Environmental Quality indicated in their second annual report that granting exceptions and variances has become quite common.[16] The CEQ has already recognized the limitations of the regulatory process. A single sentence from their report summarizes the case against overreliance on regulation:

It is also clear, however, that because of the enforcement, efficiency, and equity problems of the regulatory approach, other means of achieving pollution abatement must also be probed.[17]

In the United States the regulatory approach to economic policy, in spite of its past failures, is generally favored over a market approach. The lessons of history appear to have little impact on future policy formulation. The role of regulation in environmental policy should be held to a minimum.

Part Four

ALTERNATIVE POLICY PROGRAMS

11

Market Solutions to Environmental Problems

Thus far, the analysis developed in this text reflects the economist's view of pollution. Behavior which others regard as irresponsible or even immoral disregard for the natural environment, the economist classifies as the unwanted consequences of a failure of resource-allocating institutions.

When markets fail to perform their functions, or do not exist, the economist looks to the ideal market model as a guide for public policy.[1] Numerous students of the economics of pollution have devised and advocated pollution control policies that entail either the creation of a market for environmental services when none exists or, at the very least, the imposition of prices for environmental services when prices do not exist. The former approach may be referred to as the "pollution rights" technique and the latter the "effluent charges" technique. A variant of the effluent charges approach has been legislatively adopted in Vermont and has been considered (and rejected) by the United States Senate Committee on Public Works. Both approaches are examined in detail in this chapter.

A Notion of the Ideal

Market approaches to the allocation of common property resources may be illustrated with a simple model. Envision an economy encom-

passing a single river basin. For the moment assume that the economy has no dealings with the outside world. A manufacturer dumps
organic wastes into the river and reduces the level of dissolved oxygen (DO) well below that which would prevail in the river's pristine
state.

Curve MC in Figure 11-1 is a schedule of the marginal cost of increasing the quality of the stream by increasing the level of DO. The
curve is termed the marginal cost of abatement schedule. Water
quality is measured on the horizontal axis as the level of dissolved
oxygen below the manufacturer's waste outfall in the river. Point $0X_1$
indicates the current level of dissolved oxygen which will continue to
exist as long as the manufacturer continues to produce the same
level of output and to rely on current waste disposal techniques. The
MC curve reflects a choice of the least cost technological option for
increasing DO in the stream. While the option will remain unspeci-
fied, it could involve any combination of a number of possible techniques: process changes, recycling of waste water, some form of
treatment, or land disposal. The positive slope of the MC curve reflects the assumption that, at the margin, increases in DO are increasingly costly.

It is also assumed that no social costs are associated with abatement. In reality, of course, reducing water pollution by any of the
standard technologies would involve external, nonmonetary costs.
Pollution abatement, like any other product, requires power, bricks
and mortar, transportation, and other polluting inputs. Graphically,
these costs would be reflected in a higher marginal cost of abatement curve than that depicted in Figure 11-1.

Figure 11-1   The Receptor Quality Charge — One Polluter

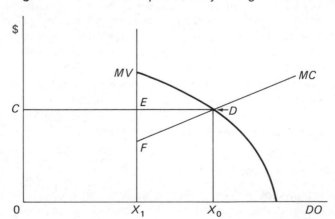

Curve MV in Figure 11-1 is an aggregate marginal valuation curve (see Chapter 8, pp. 124–126). Each point on the curve indicates the sum of the payments each of the affected river basin residents would be willing to pay in order to obtain successive increases in DO in the river. Those living near the outfall might be expected to place the highest value on cleanup. Those living way upstream or way downstream will place a lower value on the less direct benefits that might stem from pollution reduction.

The MV curve has a negative slope on the assumption that when water quality is very low, some improvement would be valued very highly and that when water quality is very high, any further increase in DO will have little or no subjective value. It is also assumed that the curve reflects the residents' evaluations of *all* uses alternative to waste disposal and that each alternative use has the characteristics of a public good; for example, once swimming becomes safe and desirable, everyone can swim in the river without charge.

Given the cost and valuation schedules presented in Figure 11-1, the best use of the river — its economically efficient use — requires a DO count of OX_0. At this level of DO, the increasing marginal cost of abatement is just equal to the decreasing marginal valuation of abatement. Accordingly, waste discharges must be reduced by an amount sufficient to add $OX_0 - OX_1$ units of DO to the river. Any greater increase in DO would cost more than it is worth, and the river basin's residents would experience a decrease in total wellbeing. Any smaller increase in DO would leave open the possibility of further welfare gains.

If social costs in addition to money outlays are associated with abatement, the marginal cost of abatement curve in Figure 11-1 would be higher and would intersect MV at a lower level of DO. The optimal level of abatement expenditures would be correspondingly less. Ignoring such costs in practice when in fact they exist would clearly lead to a tendency to overabate.

The Constraints of the Real World:
The Income Distribution Effect

On purely logical grounds, one might argue that the suboptimal use of the river, as described above, will not continue in the face of economic pressures to reduce pollution. If the MV curve of Figure 11-1 accurately portrays the basin residents' evaluation of a cleaner river, they would immediately instruct their local government to purchase a decrease in pollution from the manufacturer.

People buy fire protection through government because they see a gain from sharing costs; why not do the same for pollution abatement? The fact that, in many cases, society has *not* bought pollution abatement does not necessarily indicate that the situation described in the above model is not an accurate representation of the real world. Although the real world marginal valuation curves may intersect the marginal cost of abatement curves at or above the current level of abatement, the real world political system may just be slow to respond, or incapable of responding, to the desire for less pollution. The notion of citizens having to pay for pollution abatement may seem outrageous. If citizens own the rivers, they should not have to pay to keep the rivers clean. This naive moral position has a somewhat more sophisticated corollary. Residents of the polluted river basin may feel that they can pass the cost of abating pollution on to others by forcing the firm to meet a stream standard. The residents expect the abatement costs would then be paid for by the firm's owners or by its customers (through lower profits or higher product prices). Given this expectation, however valid or invalid it may be, the public would not consider government purchases of cleaner water from the polluter as a very attractive alternative. Moreover, the residents' notion of fairness may suggest that "public ownership" of the river requires that the firm's owners or customers, or both, pay the public for the use of the river. All these arguments are frequently presented. Yet, in one sense, they have little to recommend them as policy guides. If the river basin is a *closed* economy, as we have assumed, then the basin's residents (the potential beneficiaries of pollution abatement) are the firm's owners and workers as well as its customers. In short, they will pay whether they purchase cleaner water from the firm or the firm is forced to undertake abatement expenditures out of its earnings. The cost of cleaner water is the goods and services society must give up to obtain cleaner water. These costs cannot be avoided except to the extent that they may be exported from the geographic area in which they are incurred. In our model of a closed river basin, we have assumed away the possibility of shifting costs to others by assuming that no trade takes place between the model basin and the rest of the world. In the United States economy, which is relatively open, the possibility of international shifting of abatement costs exists, but should not be taken for granted. Competition in world markets with countries having less stringent abatement requirements than ours could prevent the export price increases which would be required for international shifting to take place. In all likelihood, the cost of abating pollution in the United States will have to be borne by United States' citizens as a whole, however these total costs may be distributed.

Awareness that the aggregate costs of abatement cannot be avoided does not vitiate the political consequences stemming from disaggregated income redistributional effects. The political feasibility of an abatement program will depend to a great extent on the program's expected distribution of gains and losses. Both public subsidies for pollution reduction and taxes to stimulate pollution abatement are on the spectrum of alternate policies and may involve the same total costs. Given the public's knowledge of cost distribution under alternative schemes, however, the tax approach will be favored by taxpayer-citizens and the subsidy approach will be favored by owners of polluting firms. For the moment, the cost distribution issue will be sidestepped to focus on the efficiency questions which the tools of economics can handle with less ambiguity.

Market Oriented Policy Tools

Each of the following policy tools involves some form of monetary incentive device and qualifies as a market oriented technique. Even those alternatives which are clearly unworkable or unacceptable are considered so that the expected benefits of market solutions will be clear.

All of the institutional techniques to be discussed here — with the exception of one variant of the pollution rights approach — are methods of implementing politically determined standards of environmental quality. In other words, we beg the question of the political system's capability of accurately weighing costs against benefits in choosing environmental quality goals by assuming that a correct choice, X_0 in the current example, has been made. The problem now is to find a way of enforcing that standard in an efficient way.

The Subsidy Approach: Public Purchase of Pollution Abatement at Value   The local municipality could induce the manufacturer to increase DO by paying him for each additional unit of DO produced by his abatement efforts. The payment per unit of DO would be the sum of the residents' marginal valuations of DO at the optimum level of DO. In terms of the cost and valuation schedules of Figure 11-1, the municipality would pay X_0D to the manufacturer for each added unit of DO up to $0X_0$ units. The firm would have an incentive to curb its disposal of wastes since the difference between MC and X_0D for units of DO below the optimum level provides a margin of profit. The area of the triangle *DEF* measures the profits the firm could make by increasing DO to $0X_0$. The firm also has an incentive to select least-cost abatement techniques (those assumed to underlie the MC schedule in Figure 11-1) in order to obtain the maximum profit. The firm would be in the business of selling cleaner water at a price citizens would be willing to pay. Although in a given case this technique would yield all the desirable allocation consequences, it must be rejected, because a public policy which made pollution profitable would encourage more pollution.

The Subsidy Approach: Public Purchase of Pollution Abatement at Cost The subsidy approach does not have to provide profit to the polluter. The municipality could purchase pollution abatement from the polluter at cost and allow no margin of profit. There are two variants of this technique. If the municipality knows the marginal cost of abatement schedule, it may simply grant the total cost of abatement to the firm. Alternatively, if the municipality does not know the marginal cost of abatement schedule, it could reimburse the firm for expenditures necessary to increase DO to the desired standard. Both variants entail formidable problems. The first alternative will work only when accompanied by both the knowledge of clean-up costs and an enforcement program. Knowledge of least-cost abatement techniques by the enforcing agency probably will be deficient. The requirement of an additional legal enforcement program under this variant of the cost subsidy approach renders the approach essentially the same as the current regulatory approach. As such, all of the difficulties of regulation will be encountered.

The second variant of the cost subsidy technique — reimbursing the firm for its abatement expenditures — has all of the disadvantages of the first variant plus the distinct disadvantage of placing no limits on abatement subsidies. The manufacturer will have no incentive to minimize abatement costs in attaining the water quality standard. The well-known difficulties of cost control in defense procurement suggest the deficiencies of the cost-plus approach. For this reason, most economists would reject this form of subsidy.

Public Purchase of Pollution Abatement at Cost — The Public Service Approach In some cases the government could construct and operate abatement facilities.[2] For example, the government agency might intercept and treat effluents to the optimal DO level. If both capital and current expenditures were financed out of the government budget, the public service approach would be, in most respects, the same as the cost subsidy approach with a known marginal cost of abatement. The difference, of course, would lie in the fact that governmental supervision would be direct and ongoing rather than after the fact.

Public production of pollution abatement permits a variety of financing arrangements which will influence the distribution of abatement costs as well as the efficiency of waste management. As an alternative to financing expenditures through direct taxes on river basin residents, indirect taxes may be levied on polluters in the form of user charges. The user charge would be an annual fee equal to the annual capital costs plus the operating costs of the abatement facility. User charges for publicly constructed facilities are appealing for several reasons. In the first place, user charges have the apparent advantage of fairness: in a perfectly competitive market system, consumers of polluting products would pay through higher prices the cost of abating pollution. User charges are also desirable in terms of efficiency. On the one hand, if the consumer has to pay for abatement costs in the price of the products he purchases, he will adjust his consumption of those commodities to more accurately reflect their true cost. The same argument applies, of course, to any abatement financing scheme that places the initial burden of abatement costs on producers. On the other hand, the user charge approach has the added advantage of limiting the amount of knowledge required by governmental authorities in establishing effective antipollution programs. The government agency need only concern itself with those abatement alternatives which have the advantage of economies of scale, for example, joint treatment, aeration, or flow augmentation in the case of water quality control. Levying a user charge for the public abatement facility would encourage firms to seek out their own cheaper alternatives.[3] To avoid wasteful expenditures on public facilities that might go unused if polluters find less costly alternatives, the efficiency benefits of this approach could be realized by announcing the user charge prior to construction of the public facility. Firms would have an opportunity to explore less costly alternatives. It should be noted that this approach still requires regulatory activity. The firm must be legally required to participate in the government's abatement program. The approach also requires that the regulatory agency have some knowledge of least-cost abatement technologies.

A final variant of the public service approach is frequently used and has many attractive features. The municipality could construct a municipal treatment facility capable of handling both residential wastes and the wastes generated by the manufacturing firm. The user charge for both the residents (as taxpayers) and the industry should be set to cover annual total cost. The proper division of total cost between the municipality and the firm would be uncertain. If the marginal cost of abatement schedule is upward-sloping, like amounts of effluent cost more to treat at the right end of the curve than at the left end. There is no way of specifying which segment of the curve applies to the firm's effluent and which segment applies to the municipality's effluent. An acceptable rule of thumb might be to divide the total cost between the municipality and the firm in proportion to their respective contributions to the total wastes treated.

The Receptor Quality Charge Approach   Another method of obtaining the desired level of DO would involve levying a charge on the polluter. The charge would be equal to society's marginal valuation of DO at the optimal level of DO. In Figure 11-1 the firm would be charged $0C$ dollars for each unit of DO between the current level of DO and the optimal level. The charge would induce the firm to attempt to lower the charge by finding ways to increase DO in the stream. The firm's benefit-cost calculations would compare the cost of a unit increase in DO with the benefit of reducing its stream quality charge payments. The stream quality charge curve CD in Figure 11-1 becomes a type of marginal revenue schedule which represents charges avoided rather than increases in revenue. The firm would compare the savings in charges with the cost of achieving those savings and, as long as the former exceeded the latter, would undertake additional clean-up measures. Beyond X_0 level of DO, a further increase in DO would cost the firm an amount greater than the tax savings.

The most frequently suggested effluent charge approach to pollution abatement is a highly modified version of the above model.[4] The usual effluent charge proposal takes into consideration the relationship between the quality of the waste receptor and the quantity of wastes being discharged. For example, under constant conditions of stream flow, a known decrease in biochemical oxygen demand (BOD) is required to produce a unit increase in DO. Given this relationship, the marginal valuation schedule can be conceptualized in terms of units of waste discharge rather than units of receptor quality. For example, if it is known that a one unit increase in DO can be obtained with a hundred unit reduction in BOD and that society's marginal valuation of that unit increase in DO is $100, then an effluent charge of one dollar for each unit of BOD discharged will produce the same response from the firm as a $100 tax on each unit of DO between the current and optimal level of DO. The effluent charge system commonly suggested would tax waste discharges rather than units of quality degradation.

The only difference between the receptor quality charge described here and the most frequently suggested system is that the latter would apply the charge to *every* unit of BOD emitted and not just to

BOD causing a difference between the current level and the optimal level of DO. The implication of this difference is that once the optimal level of DO is achieved, the current model would not require the continued payment of a charge, while the typical effluent charge model would require payment of the charges as long as wastes continued to be discharged. Continued payment would probably be defended on the grounds that units of waste discharge are a measure of the use of a common property resource and that society should be compensated for that use. To the contrary, it may be argued that continued payment serves no useful allocative purpose once the best use of the resource has already been obtained and constitutes an unnecessary and arbitrary redistribution of income among citizen-consumers.

Implementation of the idealized receptor quality charge model is complicated by a number of factors. In the first place, society's marginal valuation of improved receptor quality is simply not known. Recreational and esthetic uses of water are in the nature of public goods as are virtually all uses of air. This problem besets almost any pollution control strategy. With the exception of one variant of the pollution rights approach, it will always be necessary for government to decide on environmental quality standards politically and prior to improvement efforts.

The effluent charge approach could be implemented without knowledge of marginal valuations. A politically determined stream or air quality standard could be achieved by forcing polluters to pay a charge equal to the marginal cost of the last desired unit of receptor quality. This approach is feasible, of course, only if the marginal cost of increased receptor quality is known to the government agency. If the marginal cost is not known, the government agency could conceivably implement an effluent charge based on a "guesstimate" of the marginal cost of abatement and wait to see if the polluter's response generated the desired level of water or air quality.

The receptor quality charge has potential usefulness in more complex situations; indeed, the primary usefulness of the charge lies in the possibility of dealing with more than one polluter. Suppose two firms using identical production processes and operating at the same level of production are dumping organic wastes into the same river. One firm is located upstream where the volume of water is low and one is downstream where flow is much greater. Assume further that the distance between the two firms is great enough so that DO is completely restored before the stream reaches the downstream plant. Because both plants are assumed to be discharging the same amount of BOD into unequal quantities of water, the quality of the stream just below the downstream outfall will be higher than that just below the upstream outfall. Uniform water quality throughout the length of the stream can be assured with a uniform charge on both polluters. Figure 11-2 illustrates this result. A charge of 0C dollars is levied on both firms. Although the upstream firm has to move further along the DO axis before minimizing its costs, both firms will eventually reach X_0.

Pollution Rights   The fullest use of the market to allocate common property resources is represented by the pollution rights technique. Two variants of the technique are discussed in this section. The first variant would create a market for environmental services and auction these services to all users, polluters and nonpolluters alike. The second variant — the one most frequently proposed — envisions governmental sale of environmental services to polluters up to a politically determined acceptable level.

The first variant represents the only case in which the creation of a market for environmental services can simulate completely the functions of markets for private goods. All of the methods discussed so far have assumed a given stream quality standard. Their aim has been simply to attain that standard in the most efficient way. The creation of markets for the full range of environmental services would permit the simultaneous making of decisions not only about the least-cost method of achieving a quality standard, but also about the level at which the standard should be set.

Figure 11-2 The Receptor Quality
Charge — Multiple Polluters

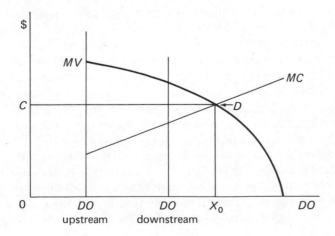

The characteristics of this technique can be seen by supposing that ownership of a common property resource is vested in a public corporation distinct from the local governmental unit. Specifically, assume that the river in our river basin model is "owned" by a single authority which has the power to sell all rights to all uses of the river. Suppose the river basin authority auctions off the right to reduce the river's quality below that of its pristine state. The rights to reduce DO by successive units are put on the block with industrial and municipal representatives vying one with the other. When the first unit is put up for bid, the manufacturer may outbid the municipality because the cost to the manufacturer of a last unit of treatment will be high but a small initial reduction in DO is not of great importance to the people of the community. The second and some subsequent unit reductions in DO may also be won by the manufacturer. Eventually, because the marginal cost of initial units of waste treatment is low and the marginal value of cleaner water when waste loadings are great is high, the municipality will outbid the firm. Assume this occurs at the sixth unit. Because the firm cannot "skip" a unit of pollution in substituting treatment for the use of the watercourse, the bidding is, in effect, ended. The right to reduce DO by a seventh unit is useless — has zero value — to the firm unless it also has purchased the right to reduce DO by a sixth unit.

This bidding would yield an efficient use of the river. The manufacturer would undertake *some* treatment, abatement, or process changes, and local citizens would have reserved for themselves the right to use the river for recreational and esthetic purposes. The distributional aspects of this bidding arrangement, however, require the manufacturer to pay the basin authority the sum of his marginal payments for each of the units he purchased and they require the municipality to make an actual payment only on the sixth unit, the unit which prevents further degradation of the river.

This particular distributional outcome would be reversed if the illustration were reversed so that initially the manufacturer was polluting the river free of charge. In this case the basin authority would be selling "rights to clean water," that is, rights to successive increases in water quality. In these circumstances, the municipality's representatives would begin by outbidding the industrial user. Again, the efficient level of DO would be attained, but the citizen rather than the industrial user or his customers would end up footing the bill.

The second variant of the pollution rights technique begins by assigning ownership of the clean river to a governmental unit. The river is publicly owned and government may permit industrial users to bid for the privilege ("right" is the word usually used in this context) to pollute it. This technique has been put forward by Dales.[5] In the typical presentation, the government decides on the degree of DO reduction which will be tolerated. Industrial users then compete for a share of these rights to pollute. Generally speaking, those manufacturers with the highest treatment costs will outbid those with lower treatment costs. The effect of the bidding process would be a least-cost set of arrangements for producing the required water quality improvement.

This pollution rights variant shares all of the beneficial aspects of effluent charges and is alleged to have further value because of its flexibility in response to real world dynamics. For example, if citizens decide that they wish to expand recreational use of the river (a not unlikely event in light of the apparently income-elastic demand for recreation), government can either buy back rights to pollute from firms or simply reduce the number of rights to be sold in subsequent periods. In either case, the effect is to increase the price of pollution rights and force some firms to undertake abatement as the less expensive option.

The pollution rights method also permits depersonalized adaptation to economic growth. New firms intending to locate in a given river basin will face the choice of abatement or the purchase of pollution rights. Again, if the cost of abatement for the new firm is relatively high, it will purchase pollution rights from an existing firm which might gain from switching to relatively lower cost abatement.

Advantages and Problems of Market Solutions

Aside from the economist's predilection for market solutions, what advantages do market techniques have over the existing system of legal enforcement of effluent standards? Two lines of argument have been advanced. First, the environmentalists' frustration with the plodding pace of enforcement naturally stimulates the search for new solutions. The stream standards enforcement approach, with negotiated effluent limitations, is seen as too easily manipulated by vested interests. Advocates of the pollution rights and effluent charges approaches assert that market solutions will accomplish two important results. The assignment of effluent shares among firms will be depersonalized and the bargaining element removed. Rather than protesting its cost share, the polluter facing an effluent charge will have no choice but to respond to a fixed cost of effluent discharge. The only way he can avoid that cost is by cutting back on his discharges. Participation in bargaining games will no longer involve a payoff. In the case of pollution rights the bargaining element is also removed. The only way of escaping abatement costs is to purchase the right to pollute.

Second, the effluent charge and pollution rights approaches will yield close to a least-cost solution to the abatement problem. Given that all firms act to equate their marginal cost of abatement to the common effluent charge or pollution rights price, no cost reduction for the system as a whole can be obtained by shifting abatement responsibility from one firm to another.

If the burden of proof is placed on the effluent charge advocates, they must also argue that the regulatory approach will not — or at least is not likely to — yield the same least-cost mix of abatement assignments among firms. In the context of limited agency budgets — and hence limited agency expertise — and the informational strategies likely to be pursued by firms, the market solution will probably not be achieved by regulation. To duplicate the market's least-cost solution, the agency would have to assign discharge permits in such a way as to equate marginal costs of abatement for all discharges. Thus, informational requirements are great and generally they will not be met. The informational requirements could be met only at great cost to the public for the purchase of expert advice.

The set of arguments in favor of a market system is very persuasive, yet it must be recognized that market solutions will face substantial practical and political difficulties. It must be assumed, for purposes of comparison with the regulatory approach, that enforcement agencies will have to act without knowledge of abatement cost functions. If these functions were known, one of the major advantages of effluent charges would be removed. The least-cost solution would be known, and only the problem of legal enforcement of that solution would remain. Assuming the lack of cost knowledge, advocates of the effluent charge suggest that the charge be set according to a "guesstimate." If the charge were wrong, it could be changed later.[6] It is unlikely, however, that a flexible charge will be politically acceptable. An increase in the charge, after abatement facilities of the appropriate scale had been constructed, would be bitterly opposed by the polluters. Thus, the suggestion is frequently made that charges should be set high to begin with to avoid an irreparable error. This suggestion is deficient in at least two respects. First, high charges would decrease the initial political chances of the program. Second, charges might still have to be increased in the future as demands for cleaner water or air increase with rising incomes.

On balance, these disadvantages also characterize the regulatory approach. To maintain a stream standard in the face of industrial development would require greater abatement expenditures on the part of old firms or zero discharge for new firms. The latter option could move the entire system away from least-cost if the new firm faces higher abatement costs. Similarly, a change in demand for clean water would also require adjustments in stream standards and renegotiation of abatement responsibilities. In contrast, the pollution rights technique depoliticizes the dynamic adjustment process.

A further difficulty of the effluent charges approach is the effect of the charge on the cash flow of the polluting firms which should be undertaking abatement expenditures. If the charge is levied immediately after passage of legislation, firms that consider abatement as the profitable response will be faced with lower after-tax earnings. To the extent that a firm's ability to invest depends on the availability of internal sources of capital, the firm's ability to invest in pollution abatement facilities will be restricted. For small firms with little access to capital markets, this effect could be significant during the period when abatement facilities would have to be constructed. In the long-run, this adverse effect would not persist because firms would be replacing effluent charges with abatement expenditures. In the long-run, the firm's survival would depend only on its ability to absorb this cost or shift it forward or backward. At any rate, potential adverse effects of effluent charges in this regard can be set aside by insuring that firms will not be liable for payment of the charge until after a period of time long enough to permit firms to act on their best decision. With this adjustment in format, it appears that the effluent charges approach yields a net advantage over the regulatory approach when knowledge of minimum abatement cost functions is unavailable to the enforcement agency. This conclusion is subject to one final qualification. In water pollution control, a substantial potential exists for economies of scale. Such economies could conceivably arise through central treatment of wastes from a large number of plants, through joint treatment of domestic and industrial wastes, through augmentation of stream flow, through instream compensatory augmentation of DO by artificial aeration, or perhaps through some combination of these options. If least-cost abatement could be achieved by any one of these, the public service approach could have a decisive advantage over the effluent charges and pollution rights approaches. As noted above, public facilities would best be financed by user charges announced in advance so that firms could explore fully the possibilities of lower cost methods of abatement.

When economies of scale through joint treatment are unavailable, solutions using either effluent charges or pollution rights approaches have important advantages over the regulatory approach. Furthermore, pollution rights approaches appear to be more responsive to dynamic influences on the supply and demand for water quality than do effluent charge approaches.

These considerations have led to the increasing popularity of an eclectic approach to water pollution control, in which regional water quality management organizations would be encouraged to use selectively the full range of regulatory, public service, and market techniques to minimize the cost of securing legislated standards of water quality. This approach is premised on the reasonable assumption that attaining quality standards at least-cost is likely to require a combination of joint treatment facilities, process changes, point-source treatment, and even the dumping of untreated wastes at some locations. The basinwide agency would have the power to choose that combination of technologies which appears best for its particular circumstances and to enforce the use of these technologies by construction of facilities financed by user charges and by taking actions — through regulation or the use of effluent charges, or perhaps even through the sale of pollution rights — to induce private polluters to make reductions in waste discharges. The basin management approach has the distinct advantage of making possible least-cost solutions to waste management. Current regulatory and subsidy programs foreclose the possibility of minimizing the cost of abatement by favoring point-source treatment at uniform levels at all outfalls. While this method may have the appeal of simplicity and apparent fairness to all pollution sources, it fails to recognize that the same amounts of discharges at different points on a river will typically have different impacts on water quality because of variations in the rate of stream flow or the volume of water below the outfall. This method also fails to encourage the use of centralized techniques — such as flow augmentation — for water quality control.

For the most part, these arguments apply as well to air pollution as to water pollution. In fact, for the control of air pollution the logic of effluent charges and pollution rights approaches is even more persuasive because the economies of scale through joint treatment are generally unavailable.

Market solutions, then, seem to present significant advantages when used in an eclectic fashion. Least-cost abatement may require a combination of techniques ranging from outright legal prohibition of the dumping of toxic substances to joint treatment of organic wastes to the sale of both water and air pollution rights.

12

Summary and Policy Statement

The motivating premise of this book is that economic knowledge can be usefully applied to the environmental problem. We attempt in this chapter to summarize the major ideas and conclusions of the analysis and present the policy recommendations which seem logically to follow from the analysis.

Summary

The Nature of the Problem   The environmental problem is a special case of the general concept of market failure. A review of the literature of market failure indicates that the theoretical concepts, though long recognized by economic theorists, have been applied only recently to environmental analysis. The failure of the market system to include in the price of goods all of the costs and benefits resulting from the production and use of those goods is at the center of the environmental problem. The ability to use the environment as a cost-less, waste discharge medium lowers the direct costs and prices of polluting goods. There are, however, costs, and it is society in general that absorbs them in the form of polluted air and water, health damage, and other social ills.

The cost to industry and government of meeting new environmental standards is high in absolute dollar terms. When examined in detail, however, total investment outlays and operating costs — even in the most seriously affected industries — are not high in terms of percentages of current investment levels or current operating costs. Given reasonable periods of time, all industries and most firms will be able to accommodate themselves to the impact of the new standards.

While the immediate impact of the costs of environmental improvement falls upon the polluter, the ultimate incidence of forcing polluters to accept the full cost of production is on the citizen either as a consumer or as a factor of production. Regardless of the technique used to transfer costs from society to the polluter, the price mechanism will, as basic price theory analysis indicates, shift the costs to taxpayers, consumers, and the factors of production.

The Constraints on Policy Design The problems presented in Part Two represent critical issues which must be considered in formulating a comprehensive environmental improvement program. While there are real problems involved, the conclusion of these chapters is that solutions can be developed which, while involving costs, require only moderate trade-offs between goals.

The problem of dealing with the victims of environmental improvement — the displaced workers and the firms forced to cease production — is difficult because the victims will question the equity of their having to absorb losses as a result of environmental change. The issue of equity cannot be ignored by policy-makers. While it may be theoretically possible for those who gain from environmental improvement to compensate the losers and still realize a net gain, assurance of equity is difficult to make in the real world. The measurement of gains and losses and the determination of which losses are indeed a result of environmental improvement, are extremely difficult tasks. The losses to labor are more easily determined than the losses to capital. Ascertaining the specific cause of a plant shutdown is not easy.

The macroeconomic constraints present identifiable potential problems. Since the direction and magnitude of deviations from expected rates of inflation, unemployment, and growth can be determined with some accuracy, policies can be planned to compensate for undesired macroeconomic changes.

The macroeconomic costs lead into the apparent conflict between economic growth and environmental improvement. For the developing nations this trade-off appears more serious than for the developed nations. The developing nations are still at the point where choosing more production at the expense of environmental quality seems desirable. The more developed nations, having the goods and the standard of living which are still beyond the reach of the poorer nations, are in a position to make a trade-off at the margin and choose slightly fewer current and future goods and greater environmental quality.

Much of the literature on the conflicts between growth and the environment has simply exaggerated the extent of the problem in a manner reminiscent of the writings of Malthus. Malthusian concepts seem to enjoy periodic revivals; fears of overpopulation and stagnation seem to recur regularly. Each time, these analyses fail to take into account the flexibility and adaptability of people. The economy continues to develop new opportunities for the employment of capital, new methods of production, and new sources of raw materials. It is easy to project trends — linear or logarithmic — but the world does not always move along the mathematician's trend line.

Current and Alternative Policy The review of governmental decision-making processes, past and current environmental legislation, and the process of direct regulation leads to several conclusions. The optimum quantity of goods under a nonmarket system, as in the case of public goods, is unlikely to be attained, given the need to appraise collective marginal valuations of public goods, the free rider principle, and the impossibility of adjusting the quantity of a public good at the margin.

Spending on environmental matters by the Federal government, while increasing, is probably less than is necessary if rapid progress is to be made in solving some of our environmental problems.

Responsibility for various aspects of environmental policy has been so fragmented that it is surprising that anything at all has been accomplished.

The passage of legislation, in and of itself, does not solve the problem. The history of the Refuse Act of 1899 is evidence that good laws produce no results unless vigorously enforced.

The history of direct regulation does not recommend this approach to the environmental problem. The review of the Ash Council Report stands as clear and consistent evidence of the failure of attempts at direct governmental regulation of economic activity. Although present environmental policy is based on the regulatory approach, new techniques can and should be employed in many instances. Complete reliance on regulation results in an adverse weighting of the interests involved and should not be the sole vehicle for environmental programs.

Market systems offer promise as alternatives to the regulatory approach. The advantages of the market system for achieving an efficient use of the environment make this alternative attractive and worthy of more consideration for use in future policy design and execution.

A Policy Statement

The development of a sound and consistent policy by the Congress and Administration is a necessary condition for the improvement and preservation of the environment. The elements of the policy design which are suggested by this book are presented in this section. Some of the recommendations are quite specific, while others are framed more as general guidelines rather than as the basis for legislation.

1. *Environmental improvement must be incorporated into the general set of social goals.* While the environmental problem is currently a high priority issue, progress in pollution abatement should not be at the expense of other, longer established social goals. The elimination of poverty, the provision of adequate housing for all, and improved health services are also priority items. Trade-offs will have to be made between environmental and other goals, and concern over the environment must not be permitted to lead to the total neglect of other objectives.
2. *The concept of general public ownership of common property resources must be firmly established.* Current use of resources does not constitute ownership and the reallocation of use rights cannot be biased by current use patterns. The environmental rights of the individual citizen must be firmly established. Individual and group suits should be used as one tool of forcing improvement.
3. *Public decision-making mechanisms must be used to establish environmental standards.* The congressional establishment of guidelines for the reduction of auto-exhaust emissions is a good beginning. The role of the administrators should be limited by the use of direct legislation and Congress should be alert to administrative agencies' attempts to "soften" the enforcement of the law for the benefit of the polluters.
4. *Environmental research efforts must be expanded.* Knowledge of the effects of various forms of pollution and pollution abatement techniques is limited. If the problems of the environment are to be corrected, all the problems must be identified and solutions discovered. Research is also necessary to develop the technology to prevent pollution at the lowest possible cost. Goals of effi-

ciency must not be abandoned in the search for solutions. More attention must be given to efforts to anticipate environmental problems before they develop, before damage is done, and before vested interests are created.

5. *All environmental protection or damage correction costs resulting from the production and use of goods should be incorporated into production and/or consumption costs.* Regardless of whether this imposition of costs is through regulation or market techniques, the policy objective should be to insure that consumers and producers absorb the social, as well as the private, costs of their production and consumption decisions.

6. *Direct regulation must not be the only method of dealing with environmental problems.* Other methods must be used as the particular situation dictates. User charges allow for the achievement of economies of scale in waste treatment and thus are a good option for use in water pollution cases. The sale of pollution rights offers dynamic benefits and the opportunity for a market-balancing of waste receptor and clean uses of air and water.

7. *Society must decide the question of compensation for the victims of environmental improvement.* Is our desire for environmental improvement strong enough so that we are willing to "pay off" those who resist change because they fear a personal economic loss? Obviously there are degrees of willingness to "pay off" the losers, but it appears that compensation to workers is justified. In cases in which proof of loss can be conclusively established, assistance such as that provided by the 1962 Trade Expansion Act may be granted to businesses. These programs should be temporary and expire by law within five to ten years. By that time the initial economic impact of environmental change should have been absorbed and permanent "pork barrel" programs should be avoided.

8. *Macroeconomic objectives must be achieved.* The need for full employment remains critical for the achievement of both environmental and other goals. When the absolute amount of funds — both public and private — to be allocated to all programs is restricted, trade-offs become more difficult and most programs suffer. The social costs of recession and unemployment are simply too high to be acceptable.

9. *Economic growth need not, and cannot, be sacrificed for a cleaner environment.* While some short-run reduction in the growth rate may be required to avoid inflationary consequences of environmental change, the benefits of economic growth are too pervasive and too critical to the achievement of social goals to

be sacrificed for the long run. Ways must be found to permit a rapid growth of output without the undesirable environmental side effects.

10. *The national effort must be supplemented by attempts to gain international environmental agreements.* Many of the environmental problems affect more than one country and must be dealt with on an international basis. Further, the American balance of payments position makes international agreements even more necessary. American industry cannot be expected to compete effectively with nations which disregard the effects of production on the environment. On the other hand, possible disadvantages in international trade cannot be used as an excuse for delaying our own efforts. We cannot allow the preferred environment-growth trade-off of other nations to dominate our own selection of a trade-off.

Notes

Chapter 1

1. John Kenneth Galbraith, *The Affluent Society* 2nd rev. ed. (Boston: Houghton Mifflin Co., 1958) Ch. 21.

Chapter 2

1. Henry Sidgwick, cited in A. C. Pigou, *The Economics of Welfare,* 4th ed. (London: Macmillan and Co. Ltd., 1932), p. 184.
2. A. C. Pigou, *The Economics of Welfare,* p. 183. It should be noted that Pigou's argument had first appeared, in part, in his earlier writings [A. C. Pigou, *Wealth and Welfare* (London: Macmillan and Co., Ltd., 1912), Part II, Chaps. IV–VII.], and that the first edition of *The Economics of Welfare* was published in 1920.
3. A. C. Pigou, *The Economics of Welfare,* pp. 184–185.
4. C. E. Ferguson, *Microeconomic Theory,* Revised Edition (Homewood, Illinois: Richard D. Irwin, Inc., 1969), p. 461.
5. Many of the articles are reprinted in one volume. See American Economic Association, *Readings in Price Theory,* ed. Stigler and Boulding, (Homewood, Illinois: Richard D. Irwin, Inc., 1952). Ellis and Fellner, "External Economies and Diseconomies," *Readings in Price Theory,* pp. 242–263 gives an excellent review of the pre-World War II debate for the advanced reader.
6. Both articles have been reprinted in W. Breit and H. M. Hochman, *Readings in Microeconomics,* 2nd ed. (New York: Holt, Rinehart & Winston, Inc., 1971), pp. 484–537.

7. Bator, "The Anatomy of Market Failure," in Breit and Hochman, p. 523.
8. John Kenneth Galbraith, *The Affluent Society* (Boston: Houghton Mifflin Co., 1958), p. 253.
9. The reader interested in pursuing this topic further should read J. H. Dales, *Pollution, Property and Prices,* (Toronto: University of Toronto Press, 1968).
10. Readers interested in pursuing this topic should see William H. Miernyk, *The Elements of Input-Output Analysis* (New York: Random House, Inc., 1965).

Chapter 3

1. Further discussion of these differences can be found in Allen V. Kneese, "Air Pollution: General Background and Some Economic Aspects" in Harold Wolzen, *The Economics of Air Pollution* (New York: W. W. Norton and Co., 1966), pp. 27–37.
2. Council on Environmental Quality, *Environmental Quality: The Second Annual Report on Environmental Quality* (Washington: United States Government Printing Office, August, 1971), p. 209.
3. Council on Environmental Quality, *Environmental Quality,* p. 104.
4. Council on Environmental Quality, *Environmental Quality,* p. 212.
5. Allen V. Kneese, *Water Pollution: Economic Aspects and Research Needs* (Washington: Resources for the Future, Inc., 1962), p. 74.
6. A general discussion of the need for economic research in the water pollution area is available in Allen V. Kneese, *Water Pollution: Economic Aspects and Research Needs* (Washington: Resources for the Future, Inc., 1962).
7. Environmental Protection Agency, *The Cost of Clean Water* (Washington: United States Government Printing Office, March, 1971), Vol. II *Cost Effectiveness and Clean Water,* p. 25.
8. Environmental Protection Agency, *Cost of Clean Water,* Vol. II, pp. 25–26.
9. Environmental Protection Agency, *Cost of Clean Water,* Vol. II, p. 26.
10. Environmental Protection Agency, *Cost of Clean Water,* Vol. II, p. 26.
11. Environmental Protection Agency, *Cost of Clean Water,* Vol. II, p. 26.
12. Council on Environmental Quality, *Environmental Quality,* (Washington: United States Government Printing Office, March, 1971), p. 218.
13. Council on Environmental Quality, *Environmental Quality,* Second Annual Report, (Washington: United States Government Printing Office, August, 1971), p. 218.
14. United States Department of the Interior, Federal Water Pollution Control Administration, *The Economics of Clean Water* (Washington: U.S. Government Printing Office, March, 1970), Vol. I, pp. 121–123.
15. Environmental Protection Agency, *Cost of Clean Water,* Vol. II, pp. 87–88.
16. Federal Water Pollution Control Administration, *The Economics of Clean Water,* Vol. I, p. 124.
17. United States Bureau of the Census, *Census of Manufactures, 1967,* "Water Use in Manufacturing" (Washington: United States Government Printing Office, 1971).
18. Environmental Protection Agency, *The Economics of Clean Water* (Washington: United States Government Printing Office, 1972), Vol. I, pp. 49–61.
19. Environmental Protection Agency, *The Economics of Clean Water,* Vol. I, p. 50.

20. Environmental Protection Agency, *The Economics of Clean Water*, Vol. I, p. 94.
21. Environmental Protection Agency, *The Economics of Clean Water*, Vol. I, pp. 96–98.
22. Environmental Protection Agency, *The Economics of Clean Water*, Vol. I, pp. 96–98.

Chapter 5

1. Clair Wilcox, *Toward Social Welfare,* (Homewood, Illinois: Richard D. Irwin Inc., 1969), pp. 308–309.

Chapter 6

1. *The Economic Impact of Pollution Control: A Summary of Recent Studies,* prepared for the Council on Environmental Quality, Department of Commerce, and Environmental Protection Agency (Washington: United States Government Printing Office, March, 1972), p. 11.
2. *Wall Street Journal,* December 1, 1970, Vol. 176, No. 108, p. 40.
3. Chase Econometric Associates, "The General Economy," *The Economic Impact of Pollution Control: A Summary of Recent Studies,* prepared for the Council on Environmental Quality, Department of Commerce, and Environmental Protection Agency (Washington: United States Government Printing Office, 1972), pp. 311–332. This study represents an attempt to integrate microeconomic studies into a macroeconomic assessment of the impact of environmental improvement. The methodology involves assessing the costs of environmental improvement for individual industries and, through an input-output analysis, constructing a vector of final demand for goods and services. These final demands are adjusted to compatibility with the Chase Econometric Model and simulations are run to derive values of the major macroeconomic variables. These simulations are compared with a baseline set of projections of the variables to measure the effects of the environmental change. Simulations are also run to illustrate the magnitude of government policy necessary to bring the target variables back to the baseline level after the inclusion of the pollution control costs. Further references to this study are made in later sections of this chapter. The reader interested in all of the assumptions and results of this analysis is referred to the complete study.

    For additional data and information on this study see Michael K. Evans, "A Forecasting Model Applied to Pollution Control Costs," *The American Economic Review,* May, 1973, *63*, No. 2, pp. 244–252.
4. *The Economic Impact of Pollution Control,* pp. 321–322.
5. *The Economic Impact of Pollution Control,* pp. 321–323.
6. *The Economic Impact of Pollution Control,* pp. 321–330.
7. *The Economic Impact of Pollution Control,* pp. 321–322.
8. *The Economic Impact of Pollution Control,* pp. 326–330.

Chapter 7

1. Paul Samuelson, *Economics,* 8th edition (New York: McGraw-Hill Book Co., 1970), p. 793.

2. Although this part of the chapter specifically singles out the United States for illustrative purposes, much of what is said in this section applies to the other industrialized nations of the world who have demonstrated a remarkable capacity to duplicate the United States' growth path and problems.
3. Adam Smith, *An Inquiry into the Nature and Causes of the Wealth of Nations,* Book IV, Chapter 2 (New York: Random House, Modern Library, 1937), p. 423.
4. E. J. Mishan, *The Costs of Economic Growth* (New York: Frederick A. Praeger, 1967), p. 171.
5. W. W. Rostow, *The Stages of Economic Growth* (London: Cambridge University Press, 1961).
6. Donella H. Meadows, Dennis L. Meadows, Jorgen Randers, and William W. Behrens III, *The Limits to Growth* (New York: Universe Books, 1972).
7. *The Limits to Growth,* pp. 163–165.
8. *The Limits to Growth,* p. 192.

Chapter 8

1. John Maynard Keynes, *The General Theory of Employment, Interest, and Money* (New York: Harcourt, Brace, and Co., 1936).
2. The evolution of the "public goods" concept and of the public expenditure theories based on that concept are traced in Richard A. Musgrave, *The Theory of Public Finance* (New York: McGraw-Hill, 1959), Ch. 4.
3. A social choice model similar to the one presented here is developed by James A. Buchanan, *The Demand and Supply of Public Goods* (Chicago: Rand McNally, 1968).
4. The federal policy-making process and the budgeting process in particular conform closely to the "incremental" model described in Charles E. Lindblom, "Decision-making in Taxation and Expenditures," in Universities-National Bureau of Economic Research, *Public Finances: Needs, Sources, and Utilization* (Princeton: Princeton University Press, 1961), pp. 295–329.
5. A complete discussion of the political elements of the budgetary process is given in Aaron Wildavsky, *The Politics of the Budgetary Process* (Boston: Little, Brown and Co., 1964).
6. Aaron Wildavsky, *The Politics of the Budgetary Process.*
7. Charles E. Lindblom, "Decision-Making," p. 311.
8. Charles E. Lindblom, "Decision-Making," p. 310.

Chapter 9

1. The general outline of this history of air and water pollution control legislation is based primarily on successive issues of *Congressional Quarterly Almanac,* Vols. 18–25 (1960–1967), (Washington: Congressional Quarterly, Inc.)
2. 26 Stat. 453, *U.S. Statutes at Large.*
3. 30 Stat. 1152, *U.S. Statutes at Large.*
4. David Zwick and Marcy Benstock, eds., *Water Wasteland, Ralph Nader's Study Group Report on Water Pollution* (New York: Grossman Publishers, 1971), p. 286.
5. Charles J. Meyers and A. Dan Tarlock, *Selected Legal and Economic As-*

pects of Environmental Protection (Mineola, N.Y.: The Foundation Press, 1971), p. 160–72.

6. 37 Stat. 309, *U.S. Statutes at Large.*
7. 43 Stat. 604, *U.S. Statutes at Large.*
8. 62 Stat. 1155, *U.S. Statutes at Large.*
9. 70 Stat. 498, *U.S. Statutes at Large.*
10. *Congressional Quarterly Almanac* (1960), p. 250.
11. *Congressional Quarterly Almanac* (1960), p. 250.
12. 75 Stat. 204, *U.S. Statutes at Large.*
13. *Congressional Quarterly Almanac* (1965), p. 747.
14. 79 Stat. 903, *U.S. Statutes at Large.*
15. *Congressional Quarterly Almanac* (1965), p. 743.
16. 79 Stat. 909, *U.S. Statutes at Large.*
17. Zwick and Benstock, *Water Wasteland*, p. 287.
18. Council on Environmental Quality, *Environmental Quality,* Second Annual Report (Washington: United States Government Printing Office, 1971), p. 11.
19. *Congressional Quarterly Almanac* (1967), p. 877.
20. *Congressional Quarterly Almanac* (1966), p. 883.
21. In the spring of 1973 the Environmental Protection Agency Administrator exercised his option of extending the deadline for the 1975 standards to 1976, imposing less stringent interim standards for 1975.
22. The proposed regulations can be found in *Federal Register* (Washington: United States Government Printing Office, Vol. 37, No. 36, February 23, 1972), pp. 3882–3884.
23. Barry Newman, "Sulphur Tax: A Break for Smelters," *Wall Street Journal,* Vol. 179, No. 34, February 17, 1972, p. 14.
24. *The Washington Post,* February 19, 1972, p. A8.
25. *The Washington Post,* February 19, 1972, p. A8.
26. Council on Environmental Quality (1970), p. 44.
27. J. Clarence Davies III, *The Politics of Pollution* (New York: Western Publishing Co., 1970), p. 170.
28. Davies, *Politics of Pollution,* p. 170.
29. Zwick and Benstock, *Water Wasteland,* p. 270.
30. Zwick and Benstock, *Water Wasteland,* pp. 271–272.
31. Council on Environmental Quality, (1971), p. 217.
32. Council on Environmental Quality, (1971), p. 218.
33. Council on Environmental Quality (1971), pp. 212–213.
34. Comptroller General of the United States, *Examination Into the Effectiveness of the Construction Grant Program for Abating, Controlling and Preventing Water Pollution* (Washington: United States Government Printing Office, 1969), p. 13.
35. Comptroller General, *Examination of Construction Grant Program,* p. 13.
36. Council on Environmental Quality (1971), p. 147.
37. Comptroller General, *Examination of Construction Grant Program,* p. 48.
38. Comptroller General, *Examination of Construction Grant Program,* p. 48 (italics added)
39. Comptroller General, *Examination of Construction Grant Program,* p. 74.
40. Council on Environmental Quality (1971), p. 111.
41. Council on Environmental Quality (1971), p. 111.
42. Council on Environmental Quality (1971), p. 111.
43. Council on Environmental Quality (1971), p. 111.

44. Council on Environmental Quality (1971), p. 111.
45. 86 Stat. 816, *U.S. Statutes at Large.*
46. 86 Stat. 845, *U.S. Statutes at Large.*
47. 86 Stat. 845 and 86 Stat. 834, *U.S. Statutes at Large.*
48. 86 Stat. 860, *U.S. Statutes at Large.*
49. 86 Stat. 888, *U.S. Statutes at Large.*

Chapter 10

1. Joseph L. Sax, *Defending the Environment, A Strategy for Citizen Action* (New York: Alfred A. Knopf, Inc., 1970).
2. Sax, *Defending the Environment,* p. 167.
3. Sax, *Defending the Environment,* Ch. 8.
4. Comprehensive analyses of regulatory commissions can be found in "Final Report of the Attorney General's Committee on Administrative Procedure," (Washington: United States Government Printing Office, 1941); J. Anderson "The Emergence of the Modern Regulatory State," (Washington: Public Affairs Press, 1962); and Clair Wilcox, *Public Policies Toward Business* (Homewood, Ill.: Richard D. Irwin, Inc., 1966).
5. The President's Advisory Council on Executive Organization, *A New Regulatory Framework: Report on Selected Independent Regulatory Agencies,* (Washington: United States Government Printing Office, 1971), p. 13.
6. The President's Advisory Council, *A New Regulatory Framework,* (Washington), p. 13.
7. John R. Meyer, Merton J. Peck, John Stenason, and Charles Zwick, *The Economics of Competition in the Transportation Industries* (Cambridge: Harvard University Press, 1966), p. 273. The negative impact of inefficient regulatory policy on transportation innovation in the case of railroads is discussed and documented in Paul W. MacAvoy and James Sloss, *Regulation of Transport Innovation* (New York: Random House, 1967).
8. The President's Advisory Council, *A New Regulatory Framework,* p. 25.
9. For a review of the Ash Report, see Roger Noll, *Reforming Regulation: An Evaluation of the Ash Council Proposals,* (Washington: The Brookings Institution, 1971).
10. Noll, *Reforming Regulation,* pp. 110–111.
11. Lee Loevinger, "Regulation and Competition as Alternatives," *The Antitrust Bulletin,* January–April, 1966, p. 137.
12. Loevinger, "Regulation and Competition," p. 119.
13. Loevinger, "Regulation and Competition, p. 119.
14. A description of public policy in the oil industry can be found in United States Senate, Subcommittee on Antitrust and Monopoly, "Statement of Walter J. Mead," *Government Intervention in the Market Mechanism Part I* (Washington: United States Government Printing Office, March, 1969), pp. 77–102. A more comprehensive review of the industry can be found in M. deChazeau and A. Kahn, *Integration and Competition in the Petroleum Industry* (New Haven: Yale University Press, 1959).
15. Loevinger, "Regulation and Competition," p. 123.
16. Council on Environmental Quality, *Environmental Quality,* (Washington: United States Government Printing Office, August, 1971), p. 136.
17. Council on Environmental Quality, *Environmental Quality,* pp. 136–137.

Chapter 11

1. The seminal presentation of most of the issues developed here appears in Allen V. Kneese and Blair T. Bower, *Managing Water Quality: Economics, Technology, Institutions* (Baltimore: The Johns Hopkins Press, 1968).
2. The argument for a coordinated regional approach to water quality management and alternative methods of financing regional management systems are thoroughly dealt with in Allen Kneese, *The Economics of Regional Water Quality Management* (Baltimore: The Johns Hopkins Press, 1964).
3. This point is stressed by A. Myrick Freeman III and Robert H. Haveman, "Water Pollution Control, River Basin Authorities, and Economic Incentives," *Public Policy* XIX (Winter, 1971), pp. 53–74.
4. See Kneese and Bower, *Managing Water Quality,* Ch. 7.
5. J. H. Dales, *Pollution, Property and Prices* (Toronto: University of Toronto Press, 1968), pp. 77–100.
6. Freeman and Haveman, "Water Pollution Control," p. 72.

Index